1,417 DAYS IN REBELLION

A History of the 19th Georgia Regiment

ALLAN C. PAYTON

ISBN 979-8-88851-480-1 (Paperback)
ISBN 979-8-88851-481-8 (Digital)

First Edition

Covenant Books
11661 Hwy 707
Murrells Inlet, SC 29576
www.covenantbooks.com

To the memory of the members of the 19th Georgia Infantry,
organized in June 1861,
Confederate States of America

But some of these times all of our ghosts will get together yet,
some moonlight night, and march and camp and pick up
arms and issue ammunition around those old Virginia roads
and battle fields, just to revive once more the sentiments of
those old days, which even our ghosts will love to do.

—E. Porter Alexander, *Fighting for the Confederacy*

PREFACE

The War of the Rebellion, fought more than 150 years ago, still stings for many Southerners today. The cannons still roar, and the muskets still crack because the war was fought here. Many of us can take a short drive and visit the site of a Civil War battlefield. Some can step out the back door of our homes for the same experience. All of us have stories that have been passed down through the ages about the struggles of families during this difficult time in our history.

The attacks on Southern heritage going on today are very sad and disheartening. The memory of our loved ones deserves to be embraced on both sides of the struggle, and any attempt to erase the sacrifice of one side because it is not politically correct is a travesty. The political thought of today does not fit into the political views of the nineteenth century.

The issue of politics is not the subject of this work and will not be discussed any further. My sentiment on the subject of Southern heritage is one of preservation. I think freed slave Frederick Douglass said it best in his speech to the crowd gathered at Arlington National Cemetery on Decoration Day, May 30, 1871: "I say, if this war is to be forgotten, I ask, in the name of all things sacred, what shall men remember?"

Until a few years ago, my concept of the War Between the States, the War of the Rebellion, the Civil War, the War of Northern Aggression, or whatever name you choose was that of a distant memory—a subject relegated to classes on US history, dusty old monuments, and certain special interest groups. It had no real relevance in my life. I knew I had relatives who had fought and died in the war, but that was about as far as it went.

I found a job that required about three hours a day in commuting time. I grew weary of the news talk shows and the noise they call music today. In my search for something else to occupy my thoughts while commuting, I stumbled across a podcast called *The Civil War, (1861–1865): A History Podcast*. It is produced by a couple from their home in Colorado. The two make an excellent team. For the first time, I experienced the stories of the battles and excerpts from eyewitness accounts in a whole new way.

I never knew there was so much information available if you knew where to look. I then became obsessed with "the War" and read every book I could find on the army of Northern Virginia. I found that two of my great-great-great-grandfathers and a great-great-great-uncle were in the famous Light Division under Ambrose Powell Hill. I also found I had a great-great-great-uncle in the 7th Georgia Infantry. He was killed on the first day of the battle of Second Manassas—Bull Run for those in the north.

I could actually track some of the movements of the regiments and positions in the battle lines. My obsession grew increasingly stronger. One of my great-great-great-grandfathers was in the 35th Georgia. There is a book written by John J. Fox called *Red Clay to Richmond*, and it covered the daily life and movements of the 35th in the four-year struggle.

I wanted to do the same for the 19th.

Imagine if you will a group of men from small rural towns in west central Georgia, who had probably not traveled more than ten miles or so from their homes prior to the summer of 1861. They were sent to a training camp in what is now Kennesaw, northwest of Atlanta. After a few weeks of training, they went to Lynchburg, Virginia, on the cars—what they called the train in the nineteenth century. Moving from Lynchburg to Manassas, Virginia, to Occoquan, Virginia, they then beat a retreat to Fredericksburg. From Fredericksburg, the regiment was sent to Yorktown on the James River. After Yorktown, there was Williamsburg, followed by rear guard fighting all the way back to Richmond.

From Richmond, the 19th Georgia headed back to Manassas and then to Frederick, Maryland, and to Harpers Ferry, West Virginia, and Sharpsburg, Maryland. From Sharpsburg to Fredericksburg, the 19th Georgia was the only regiment to lose its colors. From Fredericksburg, the 19th Georgia went to Chancellorsville and then to Charleston, South Carolina, and to Lake City, Florida. The last leg of their military journey was from Florida back to Charleston, then to Petersburg, Virginia, and finally to North Carolina.

The sheer distances covered, added with their engagements in battle, create an amazing story. The following pages are not fiction. In many instances, I did have to draw my own conclusions, always basing my analysis on the research material. This is all for the 19th Georgia. Deo Vindice!

ACKNOWLEDGMENTS

The danger in attempting to thank everyone who provided assistance in this endeavor is leaving someone out. I hope I do not forget anyone.

I first want to thank my wife, Paige, for her unending support, including countless hours of traveling to battlefields, walking the trails, getting lost on the unfinished railroad cut at Manassas, Virginia, and time spent reading and writing.

Thanks to my battlefield traveling friends Banks and Jennie Freeman. Thank you to my history-loving friends in the William Thomas Overby Camp of the Sons of Confederate Veterans (SCV), including our late commander Mike Webb.

Dr. Keith Bohannon, University of West Georgia, an expert on Georgia troops in the war, provided invaluable assistance and content. Greg Biggs, with his knowledge and expertise on Confederate flags, was a tremendous help. Winston Skinner provided the first read-through edit. Greg C. White provided information and additional resources and a big dose of encouragement. John J. Fox, author of *Red Clay to Richmond*, a history of the 35th Georgia, provided guidance and assistance.

Finally, I want to thank Rich and Tracy Youngdahl, hosts of *The Civil War (1861–1865): A History Podcast*, for the great storylines, book recommendations, and even answering a few of my questions along the way.

19TH GEORGIA TIMELINE

|-June 1861 formation at Camp McDonald, Big Shanty, Kennesaw, Georgia

|—August 1861 mustered into service in the CSA Army Lynchburg, Virginia, Camp Davis

|—-September 1861 sent to Manassas Junction, Virginia, at Camp Pickens, Under Wade Hampton

|——Sent to Camp Johnson near Occoquan, Virginia,

|—-March 8, 1862 withdrawn from Northern Virginia to Camp Bartow near Fredericksburg, Virginia

|—-April 8, 1862 camped near Ashland, Virginia

|———May 1862 marched to Yorktown, Virginia

|———May 6, 1862 Battle of Etham's Landing

|———May 18, 1862 back in camp within two miles of Richmond

|———May 31, 1862 Battle of Seven Pines

|——June 1862 19th Georgia reassigned to James Archers Brigade, A. P. Hill's Division

|——June 26, 1862 Battle of Mechanicsville, also called Battle of Beaver Dam Creek

|——June 27, 1862 Battle of Gaines' Mill

|——June 30, 1862 Battle of Glendale or Frazier's Farm

|———August 9, 1862 Battle of Cedar Mountain, Virginia, also known as Slaughter Mountain

|———August 27, 1862 arrived at Manassas Junction

|———August 29 and 30, 1862 Battle of Second Manassas

|——September 1, 1862 Battle of Chantilly

|——September 4, 1862 Chantilly to Leesburg

|——September 6, 1862 crossed the Potomac into Maryland

|——September 7, 1862 bivouacked near Fredrick, Maryland

|——September 11, 1862 left Fredrick, Maryland, on march to Harpers Ferry
|——September 14, 1862 participated in the siege of Harpers Ferry stationed on Bolivar Heights
|——September 17, 1862 marched at the double-quick to Sharpsburg, Maryland. Arrived at the Antietam Battle about 4:00 p.m.
|——September 18, 1862 withdrawal from Sharpsburg, Maryland, back across the Potomac under cover of darkness
|——September 19, 1862 Battle of Shepherdstown
|——September 20, 1862 marched to Camp Bunker Hill near Winchester
|—October 1862 marched to Berryville, east of Winchester
|——November 2 and 3, 1862 Battle of Castleman's Ferry
|——November 1862 marched to Fredericksburg, Virginia
|—December 11, 1862 arrived at Thomas Yerby Estate, Belvoir
|—December 12, 1862 marched to Prospect Hill, south of Fredericksburg, near Hamilton's Crossing
|—December 13, 1862 Battle of Fredericksburg
|——April 1863 19th Georgia reassigned to Alfred Colquitt's Brigade, Robert Rodes Division
|—May 2, 1862 19th Georgia was sent on General Jackson's flanking march around Hooker's right flank, Howards Division
|—May 2, 1863 Battle of Chancellorsville
|—May 1863 19th sent to Kinston, North Carolina, at the request of D. H. Hill
|——July 9, 1863 19th Georgia ordered to Charleston, South Carolina, at Camp Johnson
|——July 16, 1863 Battle of Grimball's Landing
|——July 1863–February 1864 garrison duty at Battery Wagner and Fort Sumter
|—February 8, 1864 19th transferred from Charleston to Savannah
|—February 16, 1864 19th left Savannah for Madison, Florida, via the Florida, Atlantic, Gulf Coast Railroad
|—February 18, 1864 arrived at Olustee, Florida (approximate strength: 10 companies, 591 men)
|—February 20, 1864 Battle of Olustee

|—May 1864 took the cars back to Charleston
|—May 1864 marched back to Richmond
|—May 15, 1864 Battle of Drewery's Bluff on the James River
|—May 31, 1864 Battle of Cold Harbor
|——June 1864 returned to Petersburg trenches; Hoke's Division placed under Henry Heath
|—July 30, 1864 Battle at the Crater
|—August 18–19, 1864 Battle of Globe Tavern
|—August 21–24, 1864 Battle of Weldon Railroad
|—August 24–December 20, 1864 Battle of Petersburg
——September 30, 1864 Battle of Fort Harrison
|—December 20, 1864 took the cars to Wilmington, North Carolina
|——January 15, 1865 Battle of Fort Fisher
|—January 16, 1865 retreat to Kinston, North Carolina
|—March 8, 1865 engagement at Kinston, North Carolina
|—March 19, 1865 Battle of Bentonville, North Carolina
|—March 20, 1865 retreat to Durham, North Carolina
|——April 26, 1865 surrender at Durham Station, North Carolina

CHAPTER 1

Formation and Departure

It was summertime in Georgia in 1861, and the only thing hotter than the weather was the heated rhetoric from Washington and Richmond. Both sides began positioning for what most thought would be short conflict. The Federal government was confident the rebellious Southerners could be contained in relatively short order while the Confederate government thought independence could be achieved in one decisive battle.

Both sides soon glimpsed into the future and realized the struggle would be anything but short. The first major battle in the eastern theater was just over a month away, when the 19th Georgia Infantry was formed in June 1861.

The First Battle of Manassas was fought on July 21, 1861, as the green recruits on both sides engaged in a seesaw contest that ended in a rout of the Yankees by the rebels. The crucible experienced by both armies at Manassas Junction, Virginia, was only a hint of things to come. The battle claimed almost five thousand casualties—three thousand Union and 1,750 Confederate.

The 19th was originally known as the Second Regiment, Fourth Brigade, Georgia State Troops while at Camp McDonald. The camp was located at Big Shanty, now known as Kennesaw. The first colonel was William W. Boyd. He left with the Second Regiment on August 5–6, headed for Lynchburg, Virginia.

According to the lithograph published in 1861 by Franklin Printing House, there were a total of 743 men in the Second Regiment. The largest group within the unit was Company K, the Kingston Volunteers from Bartow County, with eighty-two men, rank and file. The smallest company was Company A, the Georgia Volunteers from Fulton County, with sixty-five men, rank and file.

The average age of soldiers in most companies was from twenty-one to twenty-six years old. Company G from Henry County had the oldest average age of twenty-six. The average height of the men in most companies was five feet, nine inches.

At Camp McDonald, the regiment went into its first training exercises. The camp was really a tent city where the raw recruits were trained in basic military procedure. The site was chosen for a couple of strategic reasons: (1) there were two streams on the sixty-acre site to serve as a freshwater source; and (2) it was near the railroad, allowing for easy transport of troops. The camp was named after a recently deceased former governor of Georgia, Charles J. McDonald.

The camp is estimated to have been the training grounds for between thirteen thousand to sixteen thousand troops. The camp was destroyed by Sherman's troops in 1864. Only five acres of the original sixty have been preserved.

Camp McDonald Marker

The regiment was made up of ten brigades from the rural counties in northwest and central Georgia. The units are as follows:

Company A—Fulton County, Georgia—Georgia Volunteers
Company B—Fulton County, Georgia—Jackson Guards
Company C—Campbell County, Georgia—Palmetto Guards
Company D—Coweta County, Georgia—Senoia Infantry
Company E—Heard County, Georgia—Heard Grays or Heard Vols.
Company F—Carroll County, Georgia—Carroll Guards
Company G—Henry County, Georgia—Henry Guards
Company H—Paulding County, Georgia—Cotton Guards
Company I—Carroll County, Georgia—Villa Rica Gold Diggers
Company K—Bartow County, Georgia—Kingston Volunteers

For the young men, most away from home and family for the first time, camp life was a novel experience. Opportunities to engage in mischief were not abundant, but they did happen from time to time. On July 4, 1861, the Irish Company, the Jackson Guards Company B, had a little too much to drink. Soldiers in the company got into a fight, requiring the camp guard, the nineteenth-century equivalent of military police, to be called in to disburse the ruckus. Before things could be brought under control, the members of the company were attempting to acquire their firearms to fight from the camp guard. The melee ended before any serious injuries occurred.[1]

The 19th Georgia did suffer casualties before ever seeing the battlefield. On the way from Lynchburg to Manassas, the regiment was involved in a train accident resulting in the death of two members. The accident occurred on September 17, 1861. As the train moved along the route, the first third of the train uncoupled. The front section continued speeding along as the uncoupled section began to slow until it reached the crest of a hill. Once over the rise, the back section sped along unrestrained, telescoping into the front section. One of the men killed was the servant of Captain Charles Mabry, Company E, Heard County Vols. His name is only shown as Murphy, 19th Georgia on the Confederate Service records. This incident is recorded in Lieutenant Colonel John B. Beall's book titled *In Barracks and Field.* On January 4, 1862, Private John Clegg of Company A Fulton County drowned. He was ice-skating on a pond near Camp Johnson near Manassas, Virginia, and fell through a weak spot in the ice. Incidentally, Private Clegg was born in Manchester, England. The story is found in a letter from a fellow soldier and the Confederate Services records.

The following document is the initial roster of the 19th Georgia mustered into service at Camp McDonald in June 1861. The information is contained in a catalog compiled by George Wadsworth as agent for J. McPherson and Company Atlanta, Georgia. The catalog originally sold for twenty-five to fifty cents. There were additional recruits added after August 1, 1861, not listed in the document.

---

1 Richard M. Coffman and Kurt D. Graham, *To Honor These Men: A History of the Phillips Georgia Legion Infantry Battalion.*

School of Instruction Document

SECOND REGIMENT.

FIELD AND STAFF OFFICERS.

Colonel,..W. W. BOYD.
Lieutenant-Colonel,...T. C. JOHNSON.
Major,...A. J. HUTCHINS.
Sergeant Major,...C. L. HUTCHINS.
Adjutant,..J. P. PERKINS.
Acting Surgeon,...G. L. JONES.
Commissary,...A. J. KENNEDAY.
Quartermaster,..S. V. SHEATS.
Drill Master,...— FONTAIN.

Second Regiment left Camp McDonald for Virginia, August 5th and 6th.

A.

GEORGIA VOLUNTEERS.

FULTON.

Captain..............F. M. Johnston.
1st Lieutenant...........W. T. Mead.
2d Lieutenant..........F. W. Stovall.
3d Lieutenant...........Wm. Mackie.
1st Sergeant.........W. H. Anthony.
2d Sergeant.........G. L. Hathaway.
3d Sergeant..............V. Dunning.
4th Sergeant...........W. H. Owen.
5th Sergeant..............G. P Campbell.
1st Corporal...........J. M. Harwell.
2d Corporal........H. P. Shackelford.
3d Corporal........+J. T. Sherwood.
4th Corporal............J. Morrison.
5th Corboral....................J. M. Willis.
Drum Major,............H D Bellingrath.
Drummer,..................J Lawshe.

PRIVATES.

Autry, J L	Lyons, V H
Bailey, J J	McGhee, J.
Bateman, W B	Meyers, W D
Bayne, J H	McArthur, J L
Boyd, A	McCarley, J J
Bowers, E M	Nash, R H
Brennan, W H	Palmer, R
Chase, W H	Palmer, J K P
Chislom, W D	Pannel, H W
Clegg, Jno	Prince, R
Daniels, Ch E	Powell, Geo
Farrar, R P	Salmons, Lewis
Farrar, W F	Salmons, A N
George, J B	Smith, J W
Gwynn, J P	Stanton, W H
Harris, J	Stowers, E J
Hesterly, J B	Terry, J H
Hesterly, F M	Thompson, J
Hewell, F J	Toy, Henry D
Higginbottom, M	Tribbel, Henry
Hill, S J	Williams, J N
Jordan, T W	Willis, J M
Kelly, J P	Wirsen, G F
Keltner, G W	Wood, J C
Keltner, T W	Wooten, J N
Keltner, H C	Wright, R B
Keltner, D E J	Webb, J B
Lemons, R J	Willingham, A
Loyd, J P	Webb, J B

B.

JACKSON GUARDS.

FULTON.

Captain..................J. H. Neal.
1st Lieutenant...........D. S. Myers,
2d Lieutenant...............J. Keely.
Ensign....................P. Fenlon.
1st Sergeant.............T. O. Kelly.
2d Sergeant.............R. Levins.
3d Sergeant..............M. Haverty.
4th Sergeant...............T. Ennis.
1st Corporal..............D. Rogan.
2d Corporal................J. McKee.
3d Corporal...............T. Daly.
4th Corporal...........H. Workman.

PRIVATES.

Autry, J	Lynch, H
Autry, N	Lynch, P
Breen, P	Lally, S
Bradly, P	Magee, J
Butler, T	Mann. J
Burns, L	Martin, P
Boyce, W	McKeown, D
Canon, P	Meehan, F
Collins, D	McCaffrey, M
Collins, J	Malowny, T
Cosgrove, J	Maroney, Daniel
Cunningham, W	McMahan, Thos
Clifford, P	Mitchell, W
Connel, —	Murray, J
Conner, B	Nealon, M N
Dunn, J	Nealy, M
Daly, D	O'Mally, P
DuPlatt, H	O'Keefe, J
Elliott, J	O'Conner, H P
Fitzgibbon, P	Priest, H P
Gavan, P	Patterson, T
Ganon, P	Roche, Mich'l
Haverty, S	Richardson, J
Hart, J	Rooney, N
Howell, S	Shanahan, W
Howell, Geo	Sullivan, D
Howell, W	Spearim, J
Hurley, J	Wilson, Jos
Kennedy, J	Wilson, J
Lynch, J	

C.

PALMETTO GUARDS.

CAMPBELL.

Captain................J. J. Beall.
1st Lieutenant........W. H. Johnson.
2d Lieutenant.......J. A. Richardson.
Ensign..................R. B. Hogan.
1st Sergeant.............D. B. Stith.
2d Sergeant..........G. E. Crawford.
3d Sergeant...........J. A. Mobley.
4th Sergeant.. ....R. A. Johnson.
1st Corporal...........W. M. Bullard.
2d Corporal...............R. Miller.
3d Corporal.............R. R. Bond.
4th Corporal..............W. D. Bond.

PRIVATES.

Barney, G	Lockey, B R B
Bailey, J F	McMillen, J
Bailey, E H	McCurley, TA
Bond, A J	Mayfield, T J
Burton, S H	Morris, T C
Camp, Jas	Owens, H A
Clark, S B	Patman, W E
Charlton, J P K	Pierce, F M
Griffeth, Sen., A J	Powell, H J
Griffeth, Jr., A J	Prewett, G W
Griffith, J M	Rainey, T F
Floyd, L F	Rainey, R E
Hopkins, T W	Renfrow, A W
Herrell, G P	Renfrow, J M
Hollice, L P	Randal, C W
Huse, B F	Smith, W T
Hayse, J	Smith, H B
Harding, J	Sparks, G B
Harding, J V	Sparks, M
Harding, T	Strong, J M
Johnson, J R	Stephens, C W
Jones, R	Stephens, T J
Jones, W H	Tatum, W D
King, T	Watts, T B
King, J M	Wilkerson, B F
Love, M C	Weever, I T
Little, H J	Willingham, A
Leatherwood, J F	Winkle, F
Leatherwood, P	Yancey, R M

D.

SENOIA INFANTRY.

COWETA.

Captain...............J. D. Hunter.
1st Lieutenant...........C. C. Seavy.
2d Lieutenant..........J. W. Hance.
Ensign...............W. J. Bridges.
1st Sergeant.........W. T. Stallings.
2d Sergeant...............D. Odom.
3d Sergeant..............R. F. Shell
4th Sergeant...........B. S. Lumpkin
1st Corporal..............R. H. Shell.
2d Corporal............J. A. Hunter.
3d Corporal...............J. H. Gay.
4th Corporal.........J. W. Carmichal

PRIVATES.

Anderson, W B	Hicks, F H
Addy, P S	Hunter R L
Anderson, W	Haines, R R
Anderson, G W	Haines, J F
Bridges, C	Harris, J G
Bowers, A A	Harrison, J H
Bailey, E	Harrison, J R
Bailey, J A	Herrin, W J
Bailey, W H	Jones, A J
Cash, T. J	Johnson, J D
Carter, B N	Johnson, J J
Coggins, J	Leech, J
Cunningham, D	Levy, E
Comer, A	London, J J
Culbreth, J T	Morgan, M J
Crawford, J M	Morgan, J A
Crawford, D A	Morgan, L M
Cole, J M	Nelson, D M
Davis, G T	Nobles, B
Digby, C T	Odom, W M
Elmore, D E.	Osburn, R P
Elmore, T A	Page, F F
Elmore, G M	Persons, W H
Elmore, J C	Poteet, W E
Edmondson, J W	Page, G
Evans, G W	Peak, E T
Fason, W T	Russell, J F
Fall, W S	Smith, C C
Fall, J. S.	Summers, J H
Garrick, S L.	Spence, W H H
Gay, S	Shaw, E N
Gay, A O	Suggs, W
Garrison, J T	Sharp, J V
Garrison, J D	Shell, W D

Sexton, W	Williams, W L
Swan, J M	Williams, R M
Turnipseed, J F	Whatley, J
Tarpley, J R	Wiggins, R G
Waldrop, L	Woodley, E M

E.

HEARD GRAYS.

HEARD.

Captain................C. W. Mabry.
1st Lieutenant........C. J. McDowell.
2d Lieutenant............D. H. Sims.
Ensign.............W. G. S. Martin.
1st Sergeant.................J. Allen.
2d Sergeant.............T. A. Hales.
3d Sergeant............P. W. Wood.
4th Sergeant...........J. W. Howell.
1st Corporal...........——
2d Corporal.............S. H. Crain.
3d Corporal............J. M. Austin.
4th Corporal..........D. M. Watts.

PRIVATES.

Alsabrook, H H	Jackson, J M
Aldridge, W	Jordan, A H
Adams, J H	Knight, W
Ashly, B F	Kelly, G W
Almon, J B	McCool, W H
Davis, W S	Monk, M D
Bryant, W	Nixon, J A
Brooks, P H	Owens, A
Butler, P	Porter, T J
Butler, D	Pace, W
Butler, A	Pike, S
Cone, W E S	Parker, J R
Cato, T	Richardson, H
Crouch, J	Read, J W
Connell, J A	Ridley, C A S
Copeland, J A	Rampy, J A
Copeland, A S F	Simms, R B
Cox, L	Samples, J B
Collins, J P	Smith, J
Daniel, C N	Smith, J A
Davis, J W	Stewart, S A
Doster, J	Stewart, J H
Doster, A	Strickland, J
Ellison, W	Thompson, R L
Ferrell, J W	Thomas, J
Gibson, R H	Townsend, G W
Gibson, J C	Thompson, A J
Galahar, G F	Toney, H P

Galahar, J D	Toney, H J
Gordon, J K	Vickers, B A
Huddleston, J	Vessels, W
Hearn, W J	Wood, W J Y
Ingram, T J	Wallace, J A
Johnson, B F	Wood, J B

F.

CARROLL GUARDS.

CARROLL.

Captain.................W. E. Curtis.
1st Lieutenant...........A. H. Black.
2d Lieutenant........H. M. Williams.
Ensign................H. W. Benson.
1st Sergeant...........W. Hamilton.
2d Sergeant............R. C. Young.
3d Sergeant.........W. P. Campbell.
4th Sergeant.........W. W. Tomme.
1st Corporal......J. T. Bedding Field.
2d Corporal...............I. J. Parr.
3d Corporal..........W. H. Norman.
4th Corporal.........R. L. Williams.

PRIVATES.

Adams, G M	Henderson, J H
Avry, S A	Johnson, J J
Barkins, T W	Kingsbery, E J
Banks, V	Kenedy, H
Barnes, T C	McCoy, W A
Barrow, J	Merrell, J W
Bently, W H	Mandeville, P J
Bonner, J B	Pitts, M D
Bridges, J M	Presley, J
Bridges, T D	Proctor, J F
Bridges, W H H	Plott, F M
Buise, J W	Pitts, I W
Buise, W C	Reid, H T
Carson, G H	Reid, W A
Cooper, W S	Smith, J P
Chandler, T H	Smith, D
Daniel, J M	Smith, G
Dempsey, L J	Smith, H W
Dempsey, S G	Stillwell, N P
Driver, W G	Stamps, F M
Elliott, S	Silvey, J H
Fielder, O H	Thompson, J E
Gambel, J B	Thompson, B
Gladney, T R	Warren, J B
Gray, B W C	Whitehorn, Z H
Hudson, E H	Weir, J R
Hamilton, A	Walker, J

Hamilton, M T
Hembree, S
Holcombe, J D
Homes, J T
Jones, J T
Williamson, R
Willingham, W T
Young, G W
Young, A C
Johnson, J J R
Johnson, J A
Jackson, M T C
Johnson G A
Kelly, J M
Kelly, H H
Upchurch, A V
Underwood, W M
Ward, E M T
Whitaker, W H
Wilder, L
Walker, G W

G.

HENRY GUARDS.

HENRY.

Captain................T. W. Flynt.
1st Lieutenant..............H. Stokes.
2d Lieutenant..........J. R. Selfridge.
Ensign..................B. S. Elliott.
1st Sergeant.............G. E. Wise.
2d Sergeant..............J. R. Elliott.
3d Sergeant............J. W. Mosley.
4th Sergeant...........J. R. Phillips.
1st Corporal...........J. B. Maddox.
2d Corporal ....S. Walker.
3d Corporal............G. T. Elliott.
4th Corporal...............A. Owen.

PRIVATES.

Alexander, H S
Amos, R L
Allums, W J
Bledsoe, W H
Brown, W J
Bonner, J
Conally, G W
Cook, B F
Cole, C
Crabb, G H
Cook, J F
Carroll, W A
Elliott, T S
Elliott, S A
English, J R
Farris, J H
Gray, J S
Gardner, P J
Grant, B W
Grant, I A
Gray, N
Gosden, W T
Guest, J M
Gray, O S
Gray, J S
Hooten, C
Hambrick, J B
Johnson, W R
Love, M J
Lewis, L
Morris, D D
Merritt, W P
McCod, W H H
Mobly, W F
Mosely, J
Oglesby, R L
Phillips, R B
Phillips, J G
Puckett, J A
Phillips, A
Phillips, J A
Rowden, E A
Rawan, A
Rape, P
Richards, J R
Smith, S H
Sikes, T M
Sherrer, J T
Stetzer, J
Speer, J H C
Stewart, J M
Tomlinson, J J
Tomlinson, J P
Townsend, J L
Teel, A
Thurmon, J M

H.

COTTON GUARDS.

PAULDING.

Captain.........................J. B. Beall.
1st Lieutenant...............M. Edwards.
2d Lieutenant.............M. T. Pickett.
Ensign.........................J. W. Neely.
1st Sergeant................W. T. Horton.
2d Sergeant.....................J. L. Able.
3d Sergeant..................L. R .Pruett.
4th Sergeant...............S. M. Roberts.
1st Corporal.................S. J. Denton.
2d Corporal..................M. C. Check.
3d Corporal................W. S. Haynes.
4th Corporal...............W. P. Parks.

PRIVATES.

Adair, T B
Adair, H C
Adair, jr., B
Adair, W H S
Allen, W J
Bohannan, J
Brook, G
Clopton, W C
Clopton, D B
Cheek, J
Cantrell, J R
Chandler, T H
Crews, J
Duke, A V
Duke, S S
Eubanks, O P
Eubanks, F M
Fuller, H L C
Fincher, M
Gaswick, N
Harrison, G
Harrison, W H
Harris, D E
Harris, W J
Haynes, J M.
Highfield, A J
Jones, W L W
Kemp, G W
Moody, W T
Morgan, E B F
Morgan, W H
Moulding, J F
McGregor, W M
Medlin, W T
Merrill, J W
Owens, J H
Puckett, E B
Puckett, J H
Puckett, J R
Pickett, F M
Roberts, J J
Richardson, J L
Roberts, S D
Rose, V D
Sheffield, W
Tidwell, P
Turner, H J
Walden, J P
Weatherington, T C
Watson, S R
Williams, J P
Yearwood, T L
Yearwood, W K
Yearwood, A J

Jones, B	Yearwood, S L
Kilby, W S	Yarborough, J
Kemp, A W	Yarborough, B

Hazel, M	Velvin, J H
Haynes, J L	Winn, R W
Haynes, W W	Waldroop, H
Hewitt, J	White, S M
Hewitt, J M	Willaughby, J

I.

GOLD DIGGERS.

CARROLL.

Captain....................J. T. Chambers.
1st Lieutenant.........T. J. Abercrombie.
2d Lieutenant................F. A. Wilds.
Ensign.......................J. L. Chambers.
1st Sergeant................R. A. Adams.
2d Sergeant.........J. M. Abercrombie.
3d Sergeant...................D. F. Dobbs.
4th Sergeant................I. W. Reeves.
1st Corporal.................J. M. Haynes.
2d Corporal.............J. G. Haynes.
3d Corporal...................T. J. Bivins.
4th Corporal..............J. R. Caldwell.

PIRAATES.

Ayers, A J	Hunton, J T
Barnes, J W	Hunton, W M
Bevins, M	Lawler, N D
Buckner, D	Lee, W
Burke, J T	Leathers, J C
Bates, J W	Leatherwood, J F
Ballard, W	McBrayer, J C
Ballard, R W	Miles, J H
Bagnell, W H	Morris, M
Bates, N S	McRae W S S
Blackburn, W H	Morris, I
Carter, S	McBrayer, S M
Chambers, W P	Mann, T
Chambers, B D	Ruffin, S S
Cheeves, W A	Richards, J W
Crook, W S	Richards, D
Dobbs, H H	Reeves, J B
Ellsbury, J B	Robbins, J M
Fields, T	Sampson, J
Fullbright, A	Stevens, J D
Fennell, S B	Scoggins, J T
Fullbright, W	Scales, J C
Gosden, J	Stark, H H
Gray, L H	Tidwell, J W
Grubbs, J	Tice, W W
Hanna, A H	Turner, B T
Hart, W R	Vines, J W

K.

KINGSTON VOLUNTEERS.

CASS.

Captain..............J. W. Hooper.
1st Lieutenant.............J. Dunlap.
2d Lieutenant.........W. M. Tumlin.
Ensign................D. Brownfield.
1st Sergeant...............W. C. Gaines.
2d Sergeant................V. H. Tumlin.
3d Sergeant......................T. H. Dodd.
4th Sergeant..........................J. Reed.
5th Sergeant..............W. D. Adams.
1st Corporal...................A. J. Payne.
2d Corporal............J. K. P. Dunlap.
3d Corporal......................G. V. Vise.
4th Corporal................F. M. Martin.
5th Corporal,..........J. L. Campen.

PRIVATES.

Ables, J	Gibbs, W H
Ables, I	Goodnight, P
Burrow, H	Grimes, J H
Boyce, J A	Griffis, H C
Bobo, L	Garland, H L
Buffington, G A	Haynes, J H
Boyce, J L	Heard, A
Boyce, W T	Henderson, J T
Brown, J F	Huff, E D
Clemmons, T A	Holland, H A
Clemmons, T	Holland, A M
Coleman, W B	Helmes, M
Cox, J A	Jordan, J R
Couch, S	Kitchens, T S
Coleman, N R	McDow, G M
Caldwell, J	McDaniel
Dye, T F	McLane, C
Dexter, G.	Nicks, H
Dempsy, J	Nicks, G C
Elkins, W J H	Neal, J P
Evans, S	Nicks, J H
Freeman, W J	Pitts, W M
Gibson, W J	Pitts, J H
Gibbs, A	Pitts, J B
Gibbs, O	Payne, S M

Powell, J M
Rogers, A G
Robinson, Y L
Rainy, J M
Roe, J
Roe, J L
Satterfield, J
Sherman, J
Sherman, C U
Stepp, S
Stepp, L
Street, J B
Taylor, M
Underwood, A
White, R
Wigley, A J
Wigley, H A
Wood, J B

REMARKS.

Company A.

Sixty-five men, rank and file.
Average age, 21 years.
Average height, 5 feet 9 inches.

Company B.

Sixty-eight men, rank and file.
Average age, 26½ years.
Average height, 5 feet 8 inches.

Company C.

Sixty-seven men, rank and file.
Average age, 24¼ years.
Average height, 5 feet 9 inches.

Company D.

Seventy-nine men, rank and file.
Average age, 21 years.
Average height, 5 feet 11¾ inches.

Company E.

Seventy-six men, rank and file.
Average age, 24¼ years.
Average height, 5 feet 9 inches.

Company F.

Seventy-one men, rank and file.
Average age, ——years.
Average height,—feet—inches.

Company G.

Seventy-five men, rank and file.
Average age, 26 years.
Average height, 5 feet 9 inches.

Company H.

Sixty-eight men, rank and file.
Average age, 21½ years.
Average height, 5 feet 9½ inches.

Company I.

Seventy-two men, rank and file.
Average age, 23 years.
Average height, 5 feet 9 inches.

Company K.

Eighty-two men, rank and file.
Average age, —years.
Average height, —feet—inches.

CHAPTER 2

Under Fire

General George McClellan devised a plan to send the Federal Army down the Chesapeake Bay to the Rappahannock River. From there, the troops would be sent up the river to the small village of Urbanna, Virginia. His plan was to march his army the sixty miles to the Confederate capital of Richmond before General Joseph Johnston could drop down from Manassas Junction, Virginia.

Like General McClellan, General Johnston was a cautious leader. His reconnaissance discovered the Federal troop movements in preparation for the advance to Urbanna. Realizing he was vastly outnumbered, having sent General Thomas J. "Stonewall" Jackson to protect the Shenandoah Valley, Johnson ordered the evacuation of Manassas Junction on March 9.

Colonel Wade Hampton was ordered to withdraw from Northern Virginia at daylight on March 8, 1862. The men of the 19th, along with the rest of the brigade, were at Camp Pickens near Manassas Junction, Virginia. The brigade kept its storehouse at the Bacon Race Church, nine miles from Manassas. Apparently, they had a "very large amount of public and private property accumulated" at the location.[1]

Bacon Race Church was officially Occoquan Baptist Church, but the congregation and building were also known as Bacon Race

---

[1] OR Series 1, Volume 5, 533.

Church and Oak Grove Church. Three miles in front of the church, Colonel Hampton had two regiments and three batteries posted. The 19th Georgia was stationed near the Occoquan Village, seven miles from Bacon Race.

The colonel placed his men, Hampton's legion, two miles further down.

The haste of the withdrawal with the enemy near at hand required the destruction of much of the property. The horses were in "wretched order and the roads were almost impassable," according to Colonel Hampton's official report. He had 130 sick men with their guns and property loaded on the wagons. He concluded the report and the justification for the destruction of the supplies by saying, "With the means at my disposal I moved, literally in the face of the enemy, four regiments of infantry, three batteries, containing 31 guns and gun carriages, and 120 cavalries, bringing all to this point safely, over roads that were scarcely passable, a distance of 50 miles. There was no straggling, no confusion, and after the first day's march, no loss of any property. If ample transportation had been placed at my command, not one particle of property, public or private, would have been destroyed."[2]

D. D. Morris from Company G mentioned the withdrawal in a letter to his wife, Sarah, dated March 16, 1862. He commented on the "retreat we had last week, we extracted back to Fredericksburg about forty miles."[3]

The 19th went into Camp Bartow near Fredericksburg, Virginia, on March 10, 1862. In a letter dated March 26, 1862, while at Camp Bartow, John B. Beall wrote to his wife, Mary, the following:

> I don't think the war can last much longer. The struggle is rapidly approaching a crisis. The Federals must conquer or fall soon. Procrastination would ruin them. They cannot

---

2 "The War of the Rebellion Official Report," Series 1, Volume 5, 533–534.

3 Letter from D. D. Morris, Company G, 19th Georgia, 48-1-1, 1978-0052M, MF-230.

> conquer us. It is true that by beating us in one or more pitched battles they might be able to carry on the war a great while yet a year or more… Two months will determine whether the war is to be a very long one.

In a subsequent letter dated April 11, 1862, in a camp near Ashland, Virginia, Beall wrote:

> We left camp Bartow/Fredericksburg on the morning of the 8th, marched to Milford Station, took the train and arrived here without baggage about 12 last night. Ashland is a small village about 16 miles north of Richmond. Our position is favorable for reinforcing the Army on the peninsula, the James about Norfolk, the coast of North Carolina or those in western Virginia. The enemy's desires are not yet fully developed, but it is believed that he aims to strike us in the peninsula (the neck of land between the Rappahannock and the York rivers) where our forces are under McGruder.

At the top of the letter, Beall wrote, "Tell George to come and bring as many recruits as he can get. I only have 65 men."[4]

The decision by General Johnston to relocate the Confederates South, first toward Gordonsville, caused George McClellan to cancel the Urbanna Plan. He devised an alternative that would be the largest amphibious operation undertaken in American military history at the time. His new plan called for movement of his 121,000 troops down the Chesapeake Bay to Fort Monroe on the Virginia Peninsula. Once landed, his army would embark on the seventy-mile trek from Yorktown to Richmond.

---

4 Beall Letters, University of North Carolina, Chapel Hill.

The Federal army sailed two hundred miles with 113 steamers, 188 schooners, eighty-eight barges, and two hundred other vessels. The flotilla transported men, horses, artillery, rations, baggage, wagons, and tons of supplies to equip the army for the capture of the Confederate capital. The Yankees left on March 17, 1862, and arrived at Fort Monroe on April 2.

McClellan was said to have assured Secretary of War Edwin Stanton, "I will carry this thing through handsomely." This thing he is referring to is what came to be known as the Peninsula Campaign.

The 19th Georgia under Gen. William H. C. Whiting's command was sent to Yorktown, where it served as a reserve division. The march to Yorktown was difficult. According to reports, the regiment covered twenty to twenty-five miles a day. Once they came near Yorktown, the 19th camped where Cornwallis surrendered his sword to George Washington some seventy-five years earlier. There was no real active duty for the regiment while serving in reserve.

The respite, however, did not last for long. On May 3, 1962, Yorktown was evacuated as the retreat to Richmond began. The 19th, along with the rest of Whiting's division, served as the rear guard for the army on the way back to Richmond.

On May 6, the Federals were spotted anchoring a fleet of ships at West Point, Virginia, and preparing to disembark. One report in the OR estimated the troop strength between twelve and sixteen regiments. Once the rebel army had passed safely on toward Richmond, General Whiting was ordered by General Gustavus W. Smith to attack and drive the Federals back to the York River.

The division bivouacked the night of May 6 in the order of battle to be ready to attack the Federals the next morning. Early on the morning of May 7, Brigadier General John Bell Hood's Texans—oddly enough including the 18th Georgia—were ordered to advance down the Brick House and Barhamsville Roads and attack the Federals. The 19th Georgia under Lieutenant Thomas C. Johnson was commanded by Colonel Hampton to form a skirmish line to the right of the Texans. As the advance was made through the woods, on each side of the road, the men came under heavy fire. Colonel

Hampton anticipated an attempt to turn his right flank. He sent for the 19th, which joined him in the woods at the double-quick.

They had hardly entered the woods when the Federals under Gen. William B. Franklin opened fire. According to the OR, the woods were dense and extensive, reducing visibility to only thirty or forty yards. Soon after engagement, the 19th was directed to support Major Stephen D. Lee's artillery firing on the enemy transport vessels. Colonel Hampton included in his report on the action the following statement: "Colonel Thomas C. Johnson and Major A. J. Hutchins of the 19th, Georgia, behaved as well as I could desire." The Battle of Eltham's Landing was a "spirited affair."[5]

Hood's loss was eight killed and twenty-eight wounded. The Confederates took forty-six of Franklin's men prisoner. General Franklin's loss was reported at forty-eight killed and 110 wounded.

Colonel Hampton's loss was small with eight killed, thirty-two wounded, and none missing.

John B. Beall described the action at Eltham's Landing in his book, *In Barracks and Field*. The 19th was ordered to advance about 150 yards into the woods, to halt there, and then deploy skirmishers. The men crouched down behind bushes, trees, or any other natural structure where they could be hidden. The men were in pairs and spaced about forty feet apart, ordered to remain concealed and quiet. It wasn't long before the men could hear the boom of guns and the roar of small arms, at first some distance, then seemed to be getting closer.

Beall described the snap made by the rifle hammer being pulled back to the firing position. He heard that snap all down the line as members of the 19th to his right and to his left all stared down the bore of their rifles. The regiment rose and moved forward. He gave an account of the regiment taking several prisoners as they pushed on toward the river. Once they got within range, the gunboats on the York opened up on them with "showers of grape," most of the shots going over their heads and rattling among the tree branches.

---

5 *The War of the Rebellion Official Report Series 1,* Volume 5, Page 48, Volume 11, Pages 627, 629, 630, and 632.

The next day, the 19th returned to rear guard action in the march back to Richmond. The following letter was written by Lieutenant William H. Johnson, Company C, Campbell County Georgia's Palmetto Guards. Johnson gives some details about the conditions the troops had to endure. Hard marching, short rations, and terrible weather became commonplace as the war dragged on.

In two miles of Richmond May 18th, 1862

Dear Sister Ella:

I have tried everybody else save you at home them will and now I appeal to you as a last resort; if this fails I must inquire of a report others receive from those at home to keep me posted in regard to you all. Since leaving, I have written different times but have received no letter yet. I am by no means of imposing or forcing a correspondence from anyone and if they care so little about hearing from me as not to answer my letters, I can occasionally at least hear from you through others or those who seem not far off from you will answer my letters.

In the first place I must apologize for writing with a pencil, but pens and ink are completely played out with us, as is almost everything else, ourselves included. We have had one of the most severe marches upon record, not so much by reason of the distance but we were upon half rations all the time and of course frequently without anything. I came nearer starving than I ever did before and hope ever will again. When a fellow gets so he is glad to get a little parched corn or will even steal some corn from a half-famished horse, as you may suppose he is about (to use a camp saying) "gone up a spout."

Besides this morning commenced the march at one o'clock in the morning, and the Yankees were so close behind us that we were afraid to stop for fear we would be overtaken by them. They pushed us pretty closely, but were very cautious how they came up. Our regiment had several skirmishes with them, of more or less importance. In all of which we got the advantage, and yet the Yankees with their usual claims to have completely surrounded us in all of them.

In one of these, our right was engaged in connection with others. We succeeded in driving them back to their boats after a fight in the woods of several hours' duration in which by their own account, we killed three hundred, we also took sixty or seventy prisoners. Our loss was eleven killed and about twenty wounded and yet they claim the victory, say we had thirty thousand engaged while they had twenty thousand, while the truth is we could not have had more than six or seven thousand. The march to this place from our last encampment was the most severe of all for it was in the night while it was raining all the time and so dark you could scarcely see the road before you. You can imagine a large army, mules, wagons, horses and artillery passing over a road on a dark rainy night cut to pieces by thousands of wagons having just passed along and you can form some conception of that night's misery. We stopped about a day to rest, but I was wet and muddy from head to footing. Employed the couple of short hours in which we rested in drying myself rather than sleep in wet, muddy clothes.

We commenced marching again about sun up, but stopped and camped about nine o'clock. When we stopped, I got hold of a piece of cake and thought I never eat anything half so good. After eating this I took a nap and I felt as fresh as ever. But our marches for weeks, at least I think are over. The whole of Johnston's army are now concentrated in and around Richmond, and here in my opinion will be the greatest battle the world ever witnessed, here will be written tis the bloodiest engagement from the book of times.

All seemed fully impressed, citizens and soldiers with the importance of the struggle and seem resolved to conquer or die. General Letcher, in a speech at a meeting of the citizens says that if the enemy demands the surrender this city of his or else it would be shelled he would reply "bombard and be damned."

The blockading of the river channel is still going on and soon channel will be one series of impediments and obstructions from city—to the city. But I think there need be no apprehension from Richmond now.

But sister I must close. I would have written you earlier but thought you have as much as you cared to answer from Tom's letters, and besides I have scarcely had time lately. Tom and Dick are very well. Give my love to all.

Yours affectionately, W. H. Johnson

Jack, I understand, is in Richmond, will be out soon, I suppose.

The return to Richmond, by several accounts, was one of the most difficult times the regiment had to endure. Captain John Keely reported in his diary:

> We would march half a day, halt, form a line, fight a little, resume the march at dark, fight again in the morning, always taking care to give our main army time to go ahead well. We were faint from hunger, fatigued almost to death, no rest, no sleep, no anything but march, starve, fight and take the rain which poured on us most pitilessly during the entire retreat, which lasted 12 days and during this time, I assure you, we had not more than 12 hours of sleep.[6]

Once back in Richmond, the 19th moved to the far right of the Confederate line in front of Richmond. The men filed on past the rest of the army and almost collapsed from exhaustion. Here the men finally got rest and nourishment. General Johnston needed time to try to determine the enemy's next move. General McClellan waited for McDowell to move south to reinforce the Army of the Potomac. US Pres. Abraham Lincoln, however, decided to pull McDowell back and redirected his corps to the Shenandoah Valley, where Stonewall Jackson was successfully confounding the federal forces.

Little Mac had to protect his supply train moving down from Whitehouse Landing. To accomplish this and continue to pressure Richmond, he stationed two of his corps: IV corps under Gen. Erasmus D. Keyes and III corps under Gen. Samuel P. Heintzelman, south of the Chickahominy River. He sent Gen. FitzJohn Porter's V Corps, Gen. William Buel Franklin's VI, and Gen. Edwin Vose Sumner's II Corps to the north bank. General Johnston saw an opportunity to take the initiative and attack the Yankees stationed south of the Chickahominy.

---

6 *John Keely Scrapbook*, Atlanta History Center.

The isolated position of the two corps made them an easy target, according to Johnston's calculation. He also had the weather on his side as heavy rains caused the river to swell, thereby further complicating any movement by the three northern corps to reinforce the two south of the river. Johnston's plan had Gen. James Longstreet marching east down the Nine Mile Road, Gen. Benjamin Huger marching southeast along the Charles City Road, and D. H. Hill moving east on the Williamsburg Road.

Brigades led by William H. C. Whiting and John B. Magruder were to converge on Old Tavern and flank Gen. Darius N. Couch's troops on the right of the Federal line near the Chickahominy. Most battle plans deviate from the plan, and the Battle of Seven Pines—Battle of Fair Oaks for the Yankees—was no exception.

Longstreet took the wrong road and blocked Huger from getting into position at the appointed time. Rather than an early morning attack on May 31, the battle didn't start until later in the afternoon. Johnston chose to stay with G. W. Smith on the Confederate left nearer the river. He chose the location in order to observe any movement from the corps north of the river to reinforce those under attack south of it. Heavy rains again made such reinforcement unlikely.

D. H. Hill and Longstreet had been engaged with the enemy for about two hours, but Johnston did not know it. Because of a phenomenon known as an acoustical shadow—the contour of the terrain making it impossible to hear the fighting—Johnston was unaware the battle had begun.

The 19th under Wade Hampton's command received orders to move forward about four in the afternoon. The brigade was sent to the right into a densely wooded area, leading into an open field. On the other side of the field was Nine Mile Road on which the 19th filed to the left.

According to John B. Beall, while the troops were on Nine Mile Road, both Confederate President Jefferson Davis and General Robert E. Lee observed the column march past. At some point, the regiment was diverted off the road into another open field. It was here the enemy had trained its artillery with much success. The regiment attempted to take the battery from the enemy, "but finding it too heavily supported, fell back, but not until after receiving its fire and giving their own in return and forcing the enemy to resume the defensive."[7]

Captain Beall further explained the movements of the 19th. According to his recollection in the book, *In Barrack and Field; Poems and Sketches of Army Life*, published in 1906, the regiment ran into a dense wood. The rains the night before had flooded the area and made the trek through the dense wood more difficult. Moving forward, the 19th ran up on another regiment lying down. The 19th followed their example and dropped to ground. The enemy fire was more intense on the left of Hampton's line, but, soon enough, the fire was heavy all along the line.

Captain Beall noticed his color-bearer with his cheek on the ground with the flag unfurled and flying. He noticed the enemy bullets hitting the ground all around John Roberts, the flag bearer. He suggested to Roberts that he and the men around him change their position as the flag was obviously a target of the Yankees. Smoke from the guns hugged the ground, making it difficult to see the enemy.

After some time, the first regiment, the 19th, joined in the fight began to fall back. The 19th followed soon afterward. Among the losses at Seven Pines was Captain Black and Sergeant Garrison from Carrollton, Georgia, Company F. The following notice was published in the *Philadelphia Inquirer* on July 26, 1862:

> Information Wanted
>
> In the battle known as Seven Pines by the Confederates and Fair Oaks by the Federals fought on the 31st of May and the 1st of June, W. F. Garrison, Orderly Sergeant of Company F, Nineteenth Georgia Regiment was reported 'missing, fate unknown.' Since that time nothing has been heard from him, and his parents who reside in Carrollton are in deep distress at his unknown fate. If anybody in either army can

7 *Southern Federal Union Newspaper* (Milledgeville, Georgia, June 10, 1862).

communicate any Intelligence concerning the fate of young Garrison it will be conferring a great favor upon his now deeply grieved relatives. If the New York and Philadelphia papers would institute an inquiry through their columns concerning this young man, probably it would accomplish the objective of this paragraph. The service would be cheerfully paid for, if there was any way to forward the money, but under existing circumstances this is impossible. Will not the papers of those cities, for the sake of humanity, aid in ascertaining the fate of the missing one, and thereby if possible relieve the terrible load of suspense and agony under which his father and mother now suffer. Any information directed to Petersburg Express will be cheerfully communicated to the parents at Carrollton, Georgia.[8]

[8] *The Philadelphia Inquirer*, 26 July 1862.

CHAPTER 3

The Seven Days—the Making of a Leader

Following the battle of Seven Pines—also called the Battle of Fair Oaks by the Yankee—on May 31, 1862, the Confederate Army underwent a number of changes.

After the wounding of General Joseph E. Johnston, President Jefferson Davis wasted no time appointing Robert E. Lee commander of the Confederate States Army. The losses at Seven Pines caused the new commander to reorganize portions of the army. On June 11, 1862, James J. Archer's brigade was ordered to join Ambrose Powell Hill's Light Division.

A. P. Hill coined the name "Light Division" himself. The real reason for the name is lost to history, but there are several theories: (1) he wanted to distinguish his brigade from that of Daniel Harvey Hill; (2) he wanted to pay homage to the Light Brigade from the Crimean War; and (3) he chose the name to epitomize the characteristics of his brigade in its fast marching, hard-hitting, tenacious, fighting spirit.

Prior to the battle on May 31, General Archer was colonel of the 5th Texas of Hood's brigade. His brigade was reduced so greatly by losses and sickness, General Lee added the 5th Alabama Battalion and the 19th Georgia Regiment. In addition to the two new brigades, the forty-five-year-old General Archer's brigade included the 1st Tennessee, 7th Tennessee, and the 14th Tennessee.

The Seven Days Battles was General Lee's introduction to commanding a grand army. His plan to remove Gen. George McClellan from around Richmond and then cut the Union Army in two was sound, but he lacked the experience to coordinate the battles in a way to achieve his goal. The lack of proper administrative infrastructure and Lee's inability to communicate with his generals effectively—including the follow-up—cost him the ultimate victory he so desired.

The Stonewall Jackson of the Shenandoah Valley, with all of his accolades and accomplishments, was not the Jackson of the Seven Days Battles. General Lee left too much of the interpretation of his orders to the recipients. The poor performance of Stonewall Jackson in the Seven Days Battles has provided historians with a real head-scratcher in the ensuing years.

When Jackson was expected to attack, he was napping. When he was expected to be marching, he was looking for a good place to bivouac. When he was ordered to repair a bridge, he saw the task as the only thing of great importance he needed to accomplish. His disappointing performance has been the hot topic of any discussion about the Seven Days Battles.

One can only imagine if Robert E. Lee had the experience in battle that he soon developed and—if the real Stonewall Jackson had shown up—what would have happened? E. Porter Alexander, in his book *Fighting for the Confederacy* wrote, "General Lee's best hopes and plans were upset and miscarried, and how he was prevented from completely destroying and capturing McClellan's whole army and all its stores and artillery by incredible slackness and delay and hanging back, which characterized General Jackson's performance of his part of the work."

The first occasion of Jackson's "slackness" took place on June 26 at the Battle of Mechanicsville. Lee's plan was for A. P. Hill's Light Division to march almost due north from Richmond on the Meadow Bridge Road to the Meadow Bridge that crossed to the north side of the Chickahominy River. One regiment led by Brigadier General Lawrence O'Bryan Branch was to march north from Richmond on the Brooke Turnpike, cross the Chickahominy, just north of Half Sink, then head southeast to the left flank of A. P. Hill's brigade and the right flank of Stonewall Jackson. Branch was to let A. P. Hill know when Jackson was in position, at which time Hill was to cross the Meadow Bridge to drive the enemy from Mechanicsville.

Hill had hoped to start the attack at 8:00 a.m., but what started at that time was the waiting. He waited and waited and waited until he made the decision at around 3:00 p.m. that Jackson surely would be in position any minute. Hill stepped off, leading his brigade across the Chickahominy. Sweeping the enemy from Mechanicsville went pretty quickly, but east of town, Hill found the enemy drawn up in a line of battle on the east bank of Beaver Dam Creek.

Brigadier General Joseph Anderson took his place in line, north of the Old Church Road as the anchor of the left flank. Archer was on Anderson's right on the south side of the Old Church Road. Brigadier General Charles Field's Virginia Regiment was on Archer's right. Further south near Ellerson's Mill was Brigadier General William Dorsey Pender's brigade of North Carolinians and the 2nd Arkansas Battalion. To Anderson's right—the anchor of the right flank—was Ripley's Brigade from Longstreet's Division. Behind and to the right of Anderson was Brigadier General Branch, and to his right, behind Archer and Field were the South Carolinians under Brigadier General Maxcy Gregg.[1]

The Light Division was facing John F. Reynolds and Truman Seymour's brigades from General George A. McCall's third division of the Federal V Corps under Fitz John Porter. The firing started as soon as the rebels cleared the hamlet of Mechanicsville. Field and Archer's Brigades were taking heavy fire as Hill's troops were fighting alone on a two-mile-long front of open plain. Hill later commented, "It was never contemplated that my division alone should have sustained the shock of this battle, but such was the case."[2]

The action was a prime example of the Confederate Army's inability to act in concert as one complete fighting body. One of the best illustrations of the action is found in the account from Sergeant

1 Martin Schenck, *Up Came Hill*, 55.
2 Clifford Dowdy, *The Seven Days*, Chapter 3.

William Frierson Fulton Jr. from the 5th Alabama Battalion, Archer's brigade:

> In the evening of that day (June 26) we came in contact with the enemy heavily entrenched at Mechanicsville. As we came out in front in an old field they began firing on us with their artillery, and the shells passed with a whizzing sound right over our heads; it was anything but pleasant. They kept up a brisk firing, but it did not retard our advance in the least. As we moved rapidly forward across the field, making for a piece of wood at the farther side where the enemy were awaiting us behind their breastworks, a battery of our artillery, commanded by Captain Pegram and manned by a company of Marylanders, came galloping up with us and passed on to our left, the men cheering and singing "Maryland my Maryland." They unlimbered their pieces right out in front of the Yankee battery and commenced firing. We watched the duel as best we could as we hurried on to the timber ahead. All this was extremely exciting to me, and I realized at once that we were entering upon a battle. My heart beat quick and my lips became dry, my legs felt weak and a prayer rose to my lips. We had barely entered the wood when pandemonium broke loose. The artillery redoubled its fury, the musketry of both sides began to roar like a storm, and I knew I was into it now. Strange to say the fear passed away, and I no longer realized the danger amid the excitement, and I could face the bullets with perfect indifference. Reaching an old rail fence in the woods I stopped behind it, and a comrade by my side called my attention to the splinters being knocked off the rails by

> the Minnie balls from the enemy's rifles and we both smiled, I suppose because they were doing the rails all the hurt and leaving us untouched. A great millpond full of water was directly in our front and it was impossible for us to reach the Yankees without swimming. We remained there shooting at them and they at us until night came down, and then all was still.

A. P. Hill has been criticized for kicking off the battle before the signal from Branch's brigade that Stonewall Jackson's division was in position. There is no documentation of disciplinary action taken by Lee against Hill for his actions. Perhaps Lee agreed with Hill's assumption that Jackson should be in position soon after he stepped off the Meadow Bridge to Mechanicsville. In Clifford Dowdy's book on the Seven Days Battles, he mentioned an account written several years after the war by Captain T. W. Sydnor of the 4th Virginia Cavalry, a native of the area. In the letter, Captain Sydnor stated he warned Lee the night of June 25 about quicksand, south of the Old Church Road. The site is where Archer's Brigade was "clinging for survival to the smokey slope of Beaver Dam Creek."[3]

The 19th was indeed doing its best to survive the deadly fire of the Yankees on the banks of Beaver Dam Creek. Captain John B. Beall from Company C, Campbell County, was injured in the battle and was being carried by litter bearers to the rear. While en route, he saw the adjutant general and informed him, "The 19th is down there at the creek suffering terribly, with no possibility of doing any good."[4]

He was told the regiment would be recalled as soon as the general adjutant could locate the Tennessee. Captain Beall, after the battle, quoted General Archer as stating, when the battle was raging, that "the 19th was at the foot of the hill as firm as a rock."

---

3 Clifford Dowdy, *The Seven Days.*

4 John B. Beall, *In Barrack and Field.*

This, according to Beall, is the origin of the regiment's nickname: "Rock Regiment." John Anderson Richardson from Company C wrote of the battle in a manuscript prepared for a reunion in August 1912. He described the action as follows:

> Our regiment had just charged most gallantly and at great loss down a hill to an impassible marsh of Beaver Dam Creek. On the other side of the creek, the enemy were entrenched. We were compelled to halt and fight unprotected because of this marsh. General Archer, our brigade commander, therefore orders us to fall back to the top of the hill down which we had just charged. When the order was received George T. Richardson said, "Boys go back in line." As he uttered these words he turned his side to the enemy and was shot through the body, dying about an hour later.[5]

The first day of the Seven Days Battles was tactically a Confederate defeat and, in the eyes of many, a waste of human capital. Lee was not yet able to lead his army in a manner bringing all the parts to act in concert for the benefit of the objective. The attacks of June 26 were disjointed and piecemeal at best. The Light Division did the best it could under the circumstances and, by many accounts, performed admirably. Nightfall brought an end to the first bloody day of the Seven Days Battles.

According to the *Official Report on the War of the Rebellion*, General James J. Archer led his brigade of 1,228 men into the battle. He reported his losses on that day at forty-three killed and 171 wounded. One of the losses was Lieutenant Colonel Johnson, who "fell gallantly cheering his men in battle."[6]

---

5 From the John A. Richardson Papers at the Atlanta History Center.

6 J. J. Archer, *War of the Rebellion Official Report*, 897.

The 19th lost all its field officers at Mechanicsville. The list of 19th members killed and wounded in the battle of Mechanicsville was published in the *Southern Confederacy*, a newspaper published in Atlanta on July 20, 1862:

> Lieut. Col Thomas C. Johnson—killed
>
> Company A Georgia Volunteers Captain F. M. Johnston Private James Ray—killed
> 2nd Lieutenant Frank M. Stovall—wounded in the hand
> Private M. Hestill—wounded in the hand
> Private Thomas Keltner—wounded in the thigh
> Private Lewis Lewis—wounded in the face
> Private William Turner—wounded in the thigh
> Private William Gavit—wounded in both thighs
>
> Company B Jackson Guards Captain J. H. Neal
> Private Daniel Sullivan—killed
> Private William Shannahan—wounded in the face
> Private Denis Collins—arm broke (since died)
> Private James McCaffry—wounded in both arms
> Corporal Pat Fitzgibbons—wounded in the head
> Private Jackson Autry—wounded in the leg
>
> Company C Palmetto Guards Captain R. B. Hogan
> Sergeant G. T. Richardson—killed
> Private A. W. Renfrow—killed
> Private W. T. Smith—killed
> Brevet 2nd Lieutenant G. E. Cranford—wounded in the hand and side
> Private S. H. McGee—wounded in the breast
> Private J. C. Morris—wounded in the side
> Private S. A. Willingham—wounded in the leg
> Private T. W. Hopkins—wounded in the thigh

Private E. R. Patman—wounded in the leg
Private Thomas Harden—wounded in the leg
Private T. J. Mayfield—wounded in the thigh
Private J. P. Miller—wounded in the leg
Private R. C. Greer—slight wound in leg

Company D Senoia Infantry Captain J. D. Hunter
Corporal W. J. Carmichael—killed
Private John T. Garrison—killed
Private W. S. Falls—killed
Brevet 2nd Lieutenant W. J. Bridges—wounded in the hand
Sergeant J. Coggins—wounded in the leg
Private W. E. Poteet—wounded in the leg
Private R. M. Carmichael—wounded in the thigh
Private M. J. Morgan—wounded in the arm
Private Green Morman—wounded in the shoulder
Private E. Levy—wounded in the shoulder
Private J. M. Swan—wounded in both legs
Private G. W. Evans—wounded in the side
Private J. D. Garrison—wounded in the side
Private J. W. Coat—wounded in the foot
Private J. H. Sharp—wounded in the chin

Company E Heard County Guards Captain C. W. Mabry
Private James Thomas—killed
Private Absalom Dorster—killed
Color Corporal B. F. Johnson—wounded in the hand
Private C. A. S. Ridley—wounded in the ankle
Private William Aldrich—wounded in the thigh and arm
Private Pickens Putler—wounded in the shoulder
Private George W. Thompson—wounded in leg
Private James Strickland—wounded in the hand

Private W. J. Willoughby—wounded in the shoulder

Company F Carroll Guards Captain William Hamilton
Private G. M. Adams—killed
Private W. G. Driver—killed
Private W. A. Pitts—killed
Private B. P. Williamson—killed
1st Lieutenant H. M. Williams—wounded in the arm
Sergeant W. P. Campbell—wounded in the head and arm
Private S. Hembry—wounded in the hand
Private W. H. Beddingfield—wounded in the arm
Private W. W. White—wounded in the hand
Private J. H. Henderson—wounded in the side
Private Thomas Baskins—wounded in the neck
Private B. W. D. C. Gray—wounded all over by a bursting of a shell
Private T. C. Barnes—wounded in the hand
Private S. Elliott—wounded in the hand
Private W. J. Patterson—wounded in the hand
Private Martin Chandler—wounded in the leg
Private D. N. Tilman—wounded in the breast
Private M. D. Pitts—wounded in the head
Private F. A. Morgan—wounded in the head

Company G Henry Guards Captain T. W. Flynt
Sergeant R. L. Amon—killed
Private John Allums—killed
Private A. V. Upchurch—mortally wounded in the thigh and arm
Sergeant J. R. Phillips—wounded in the thigh
Private J. G. Phillips—mortally wounded in body
Private John Bonner—wounded in the leg

Private J. F. Cook—wounded in the foot
Private John Boyington—wounded in the knee
Private W. J. Allums—wounded in hips
Private T. S. Elliott—wounded in the thigh
Private Abraham Roan—wounded in the side

Company H Cotton Guards Captain J. B. Beall
Private W. S. Hardaway—killed
Private W. Parks—wounded in head
Private A. J. Yearwood—slight wound in leg
Private W. J. Allen—wounded in the arm and leg
Private J. R. Cantrell—(no wound noted)

Company I Villa Rica Miners Captain John Chambers
Private W. R. Heart—killed
Private M. Hazel—killed
Sergeant B. D. Chambers—wounded in the thigh
Sergeant D. F. Dobbs—wounded in the hand
Private W. H. Blackburn—wounded in the side
Private W. P Chambers—wounded in the thigh
Private H. H. Dobbs—wounded in the thigh
Private D. Buckner—wounded in the arm and leg
Private M. Cole—wounded in the shoulder
Private W. B. Ballard—wounded in the arm

Company K Kingston Volunteers Captain John W. Hooper, Jr.
1st Lieutenant Jos Dunlap—killed
2nd Lieutenant D. L. Brownfield—killed
1st Sergeant J. K. P. Dunlap—killed
Corporal A. J. Payne—killed
Private J. T. Henderson—killed
Private C. P. Dye—killed
Private J. M. Rainey—killed
Sergeant James Reed—wounded in hand

Corporal G. V. Vise—wounded in leg
Corporal F. M. Martin—wound in body
Private Evan Ables—wounded in arm and face
Private Leroy Burough—wounded in warm and face
Private Andrew Gibbs—wounded in hand
Private H. A. Holland—wounded in face
Private A. M. Holland—wounded in knee
Private G. C. Nix—wounded in arm
Private J. P. Neal—wounded in face
Private J. R. Sherman—wounded in arm
Private Larkin Stepp—wounded in shoulder
Private John Satterfield—wounded in body
Private A. K.—wounded in arm

Thomas Johnson Grave Marker

Lieutenant Colonel Thomas C. Johnson was one of the staff officers killed at Mechanicsville on June 26. His grave and the monument above are located on Georgia, Highway 29, just south of Palmetto.

The next morning, June 27, Fitz John Porter withdrew his troops behind Powhite Creek, not far from Gaines's Mill. According to E. Porter Alexander, "The enemy had excellent engineers and had found a new position nearly as strong as Beaver Dam Creek." Fitz John Porter spotted skirmishers approaching his position and had his artillery open up on them. The skirmishers were from the Light Division, who had discovered Porter's retreat and were in pursuit. The rest of Hill's brigade got into the action with an advance force of Fitz John Porter's men and drove them back to the main body. About two that afternoon, Hill's brigade was up to the enemy lines with General James Longstreet, behind A. P. Hill. D. H. Hill was on the left—the center—and Jackson was to his left. Had all the brigades attacked as one force, clearly what Lee had in mind, the victory would have been both swift and devastating to the Union forces. The action, however, was again piecemeal. According to Alexander, "God only knows, everybody else seemed to stand still and let A. P. Hill's division, from 2:00 p.m. until near or quite four, wreck itself in splendid, but vain isolated assaults."

Of A. P. Hill, General Robert E. Lee said, in his official report of the Seven Days Battles:

> Hill's single division met this large force with impetuous courage for which that officer and his troops are distinguished. They drove the enemy back and assailed him in his strong position on the ridge. The battle raged fiercely and with varying fortune more than two hours. Three regiments pierced the enemy's line and forced their way to the crest of the hill on his left, but were compelled to fall back before overwhelming numbers.

Gaines Mill casualties, June 27:

First Lieutenant and Adjutant J. P. Perkins—wounded in body

Company A Georgia Volunteers
Corporal R. P. Farrer—killed
Private G. M. D. Powell—killed
Corporal John Morrison—wounded in side
Private Banks Crawford—wounded in face
Private Mark Higgenbotham—wounded in back

Company B Jackson Guards
Sergeant Michael Haverty—wounded in leg
Corporal Dan Day—wounded in neck and shoulder, since died
Private Stephen Haverty—wounded in leg
Private Peter Gavin—wounded in face
Private James Donnan—wounded in the groin
Private John Hart—wounded in shoulder

Company C Palmetto Guards
Corporal T. J. King—killed
Private B. F. Hughes—wounded in shoulder
Private T. A. McCurley—wounded in the hand
Private B. F. Wilkerson—wounded in the arm

Company D Senoia Infantry
Private F. M. Ship—killed
Private J. G. Harris—killed
Private R. L. Hunter—wounded in hand
Private R. R. Haynes—wounded in chin

Company E Heard County Guards
Private James Crouch—killed
Corporal S. H. Stewart—wounded in knee

Private B. F. Ashley—wounded in foot
Private William McCool—wounded in heel
Private Hudleston—wounded in the head and hand

Company F Carroll Guards
Captain William Hamilton—wounded in shoulder
Private G. H. Carson—wounded in the thigh
Private H. T. Reed—wounded in side
Private S. A. Avery—wounded in hand
Private W. Bice—wounded in knee

Company G Henry Guards
Private John English—killed
Second Lieutenant J. R. Selfridge—wounded in shoulder and arm
Corporal. H. S. Alexander—wounded in leg
Private George H. Elliott—wounded in side

Company H Cotton Guards
Corporal B. J. Denton—killed
Sergeant B. J. Yarborough—wounded in the shoulder
Sergeant S. M. Roberts—wounded in both thighs
Corporal Watson—wounded in arm
Private J. R. Puckett—wounded in arm
Private W. N. Yearwood—wounded in hand
Private F. M. Eubanks—wounded in hand
Private W. M. McGreggor—wounded in ankle
Private B. Adair—wounded in the face

Company I
Private James Bates—wounded in side
Private M. Morris—wounded in ear and neck
Private Thomas Wise—wounded in shoulder
Private W. W. Tice—wounded in head

Company K
Private James H. Nix—wounded in thigh
Private Jacob Sherman—wounded in thigh
Private Thomas C. Thornhill—wounded in shoulder
Private A. J. Wigley—wounded in arm
Private Robert Wyley—wounded in thigh and neck

The butcher's bill for the battle of Gaines's Mill for the Light Division in total was 2,688 killed and wounded. General Longstreet said of A. P. Hill's performance, "The troops of the gallant A. P. Hill, they did as much and as effective fighting as any, received little of the credit properly due them. It was their long and steady fight that thinned the Federal ranks and caused them to so foul their guns that they were out of order when the final struggle came."[7]

After the battles of the two previous days, the 19th was, like most of the Light Division, suffering from fatigue and the loss of comrades in arms. The regiment, along with the rest of the division, spent the next two days burying the fallen, tending to the wounded, and reforming their regiments.

The Battle of Garnett's and Golding's Farm was on June 28, and the Battle of Savage's Station was on June 29. The 19th was not engaged in either of the two subsequent battles immediately following Gaines's Mill.

After the all-too-brief respite, the men of the 19th were ordered to fill their canteens, load up their haversacks, and fall in for a march. A. P. Hill received orders to follow Longstreet across the Chickahominy at New Bridge and hurry southeast to the Darbytown Road, then east on the Long Bridge Road to Glendale. General Lee recognized his greatest opportunity to smash the Federal Army was at a little crossroads called Glendale. The roads from Richmond, east to west, were much more plentiful than those running north to south. As such, the Union Army would funnel through Glendale on the retreat to the

[7] Clifford Dowdy, *The Seven Days.*

James River at Haxall's Landing. General Lee's plan was for Stonewall Jackson to attack from the north, General Benjamin Huger from the northwest, down the Charles City Road and Longstreet, and A. P. Hill from the west, down the Long Bridge Road.

Little, however, would go as planned. By many accounts, Lee never again had so great an opportunity to crush the Federal Army. Huger found his path to Glendale blocked with felled trees left by the Union Army in the retreat. For reasons unknown, rather than spend the time cutting and moving the trees, Huger chose to cut a new road through the forest. This lofty solution to the downed trees took so much time, Huger's troops never engaged the enemy on the June 30.

General Jackson underperformed as he did in most of the Seven Days Battles. Lee's orders for Longstreet and A. P. Hill were to wait until they could hear Huger's guns to start their attacks. The sounds never came. General Lee, again, saw his opportunity to crush the Union Army slipping away.

Around 4:00 p.m., Lee ordered Longstreet to attack. Thus began the sixth of the seven days battles know in the north as the Battle of Glendale and in the south as the Battle of Frayser's Farm. The battle was unique in that the armies were so close, hand-to-hand fighting was prevalent.

The 19th Georgia was south of the Long Bridge Road, south and west of the Glendale crossroads. Archer's Brigade was on the right flank of Pender's Brigade, to the rear of Pickett, and just to the west of the Whitlock house. The first wave of the attack was led by South Carolinian Micah Jenkins. Jenkins led his brigade to within about a half a mile of the Willis Church Road, the primary escape route for the Union Army on the way to the James River. Jenkins' losses were heavy. It has been said that he narrowly escaped death himself—with bullet holes in his saddle blanket and the tip of his sword shot off. His horse was shot several times, and he was bruised in the shoulder by a spent shell. Even his coat had bullet holes.

Jenkins' brigade took the battery that had harassed the Confederates in that sector of the battlefield most of the day. The Federals reinforced their line and retook the guns, to be retaken by the rebels. The 19th made it to the south side of the Whitlock house.

According to the OR written by A. P. Hill, "On our extreme right matters seemed to be going badly. Two brigades of Longstreet's division had been roughly handled and had fallen back. Archer was brought up and sent in, and in his shirtsleeves, leading his gallant brigade, affairs were soon restored in that quarter."[8]

As night covered the battlefield, the 19th remained at or near where they had stopped south of the Whitlock house. The darkness brought on a familiar sadness witnessed by both armies throughout the war. The survivors tried to rest from the day's fighting while listening to the cries from the field of wounded and dying men, calling for water and their mother and loved ones back home. The sounds of the last words of men sacrificed in the day's event from north and south was described by many who witnessed the sound as the saddest thing they had ever heard.

The Seven Days Battles for the 19th was over. A. P. Hill's division saw no action on the last day of the battle at Malvern Hill. The division was too worn out to carry on. At the end of the Seven Days, A. P. Hill had lost almost a third of his division, most in the battles of Mechanicsville and Gaines's Mill. Archer brigade is reported to have lost ninety-two with another 443 wounded.[9]

Amazingly enough, despite about four thousand casualties, including killed and wounded, the spirits of the Light Division remained high. Little Powell had developed a rapport with his men that endeared him to them.

---

8 OR, 838.

9 Martin Schenck, *Up Came Hill*, 107.

CHAPTER 4

Return to Manassas

After the Seven Days, General Robert E. Lee withdrew his troops back to Richmond. He needed time to reorganize and replenish his battle-weary army. He also needed time to discern Union General George B. McClellan's next move. After retreating back to the James River, Little Mac gathered the Federal Army at Harrison's Landing, further east on the James. General Lee's concerns were compounded by the appointment of John Pope as the commander of the Union's newly designated Army of Virginia. If Lee left Pope uncontested, Pope could sweep down toward Richmond. If Lee left Richmond unoccupied, McClellan could possibly remount his offensive to take Richmond, the Confederate capital.

Part of the reorganization General Lee made during the time around Richmond was to divide his army into two wings under Longstreet and Jackson. Longstreet was in command of five regiments, and Jackson was given two. The Light Division of A. P. Hill remained under the command of Lee himself. In an effort to try to cover two potential battlefronts simultaneously, Lee sent Jackson with his two brigades north to Gordonsville to keep an eye on John Pope. He and Longstreet remained in Richmond to watch McClellan.

In a twist of good fortune, Lee found out from an exchanged prisoner that Burnside's division was leaving Harrison's Landing on the way to Fort Monroe and boarding transports to go north up the Chesapeake Bay, then up the Potomac to meet up with Pope in northern Virginia. With this knowledge, Lee ordered A. P. Hill to go with Jackson north to Gordonsville. On July 27 or 28, Hill's division left Richmond. They arrived in Gordonsville on July 29. The Light Division was the largest in the Confederate Army with about fourteen thousand troops. The addition of the Light Division brought General Jackson's force to about twenty-thousand men to watch for Pope's intentions.

John Pope had ordered General Nathaniel P. Banks to march west to destroy railroads near Culpeper. Banks stationed his division near the Rappahannock River with eleven thousand men along with John C. Fremont's thirteen thousand, Irvin McDowell's eighteen thousand and five thousand cavalry. John Pope wanted to draw Lee's army away from Richmond so McClellan could send troops north to join Pope in defense of Washington.

General Jackson learned of Pope's movement of Banks' second corps toward Culpeper on August 7. His plan was to strike Banks sooner rather than later before any of McClellan's troops could arrive from Harrison's Landing. He wanted to launch an attack on August 8.

August 8 proved not to be one of Jackson's best marching days. The weather played a big role in the pace the men kept on the day's march. Some say it was the hottest August remembered in years. There were many accounts of men dying from heatstroke. It has been said the typically stoic Jackson even showed a little compassion for the men marching in the heat and dust. The dust clouds caused by men and beast tramping on dry dusty roads was almost suffocating.

The next day, the movement was much better, and the rebels caught Banks at Cedar Mountain—also known as Slaughter's Mountain—eight miles south of Culpeper. Some accounts also refer to the battle as Cedar Run for the creek that ran along the southern end of the battlefield at the foot of the northern slope of the mountain. Banks made the first move at Jackson, once the two armies were close enough. The battle, like many, started out as an artillery duel. The Confederates had a slight advantage with Stonewall Jackson, the former artillery instructor, playing a major role in the placement of the guns.

On the southerly side of the battlefield, lay the northern slope of Cedar Mountain, where Richard Ewell placed Joseph W. Latimer's battery. The position was great for sending enfilading fire into the Federal infantry, once the attack began.

The battlefield was mostly a cornfield from the base of Cedar Mountain, north to the south side of Culpeper Road, which ran east to west. On the north side of Culpeper Road, the battlefield was shaped like an inverted "L" with a wheat field being the vertical part of the L and a brushy stubble field making up the horizontal part. The Confederates were facing east, for the most part, against a westward looking foe. The line ran north to south with the northern line making up the far left, facing the brushy field.

The eastern edge and the western edge of the wheat field was bordered by dense forest with thick undergrowth. The topography of the wheat field, in some places, made it difficult for both sides to see what was ahead of them. In some cases, only a partial glimpse of the enemy could be seen. In others, the opposing troops could not be seen at all until they crested the hill. The wheat field had been recently harvested, and the field was full of wheat shocks. The federals used the shocks as cover during the battle.

As the artillery duel faded, A. P. Hill's first troops were making their way to the field. The first to arrive was the brigade led by General Edward Lloyd Thomas. He was directed to the right of the Culpeper Road to shore up a hard-pressed right flank of Jubal Early.

Federals, led by Gen. Samuel W. Crawford, had wreaked havoc on Gen. Richard B. Garnett's brigade on the north side of Culpeper Road. Crawford and his troops were in the process of rolling up the left flank of Taliaferro's brigade.

Earlier, during the artillery duel, Charles Winder was mortally wounded in the side by a round fired by one of the federal artillery pieces. In Winder's absence, William B. Taliaferro was next in command. The change in leadership led to some confusion in the ranks. The second division made good progress hitting Jackson's left flank. Several companies of the Stonewall brigade gave way and began to beat a hasty retreat to the rear.

It was during this melee that Stonewall Jackson pulled his sword in an effort to rally his men. To his surprise, the sword had rusted in the scabbard. He quickly unhooked the scabbard from his side and raised it over his head to stem the tide of retreating soldiers. The gesture was inspiring enough to convince some of the men to turn around and face the enemy. He then went searching for A. P. Hill.

The first brigade after Thomas, who was directed to the right of the line, was Branch's brigade. Branch took his North Carolinians east, toward the enemy with his right flank on the Culpeper Road. Branch's men rushed headlong into the fray. Next in the column was Archer's brigade. General James Jay Archer was ordered forward before his line was completely formed. To the left of Branch was the 7th Tennessee, then the 5th Alabama. To the left of the Alabamians was the 19th Georgia, then the 1st Tennessee. The 14th Tennessee had not gotten all the way up, when the brigade lunged forward. The men in the 14th were ordered to catch up as best they could.

As the 19th and the rest of Archer's brigade began to move, the 1st Pennsylvania Cavalry, 164 men, came storming down the Culpeper Road from the east, headed west. The charge was as ill-timed as it was productive. The infantry rarely got an opportunity to duel with cavalry in such favorable conditions. The movement west was checked by the Confederate lines, and the men veered off to the right—north—into the wheat field. Their path took them straight in front of Archer's men coming up to the wood line. The cavalry made excellent targets for the men heading to the wheat field. According to Robert K. Krick's book, *Stonewall at Cedar Mountain*, "The murderous fire poured into the cavalry near the road left them so staggered, one of Archer's men wrote a few days later 'that instead of running straight back, they inclined along our lines.'"[1]

As Archer moved his men east, across the field, Dorsey Pender's brigade was coming from behind and moving to the left of Archer. He moved further north of Colonel Charles Ronald's brigade that had been on the field since the battle began. Pender had his line moving in a southeasterly direction, and Archer was moving in a

[1] Robert K. Krick, *Stonewall Jackson at Cedar Mountain,* 236.

northeasterly direction. The trajectory put Pender's right on a path to meet up with Archer's left. When the two brigadiers met to discuss strategy, Pender found Archer "swearing like a trooper."[2]

It is not known if the outburst was at his men or just because he was caught up in the moment as the Federals were being driven back. Archer asked Pender, "Do you curse in times like these?"

To which Pender responded, "Why, no" as he smiled sheepishly.

General Archer reported in the Official Report:

> I moved forward with the First Tennessee and Nineteenth Georgia Regiments, Fifth Alabama Battalion and Seventh Tennessee in line, leaving the Fourteenth Tennessee, which was in rear, to come up into line and overtake the brigade as best is could. I advanced several hundred yards in this manner, obliging toward the right in order to get near the left of Branch's brigade, when I overtook its left regiment which had become separated from its main body.[3]

Together the brigades established a new left flank and reversed the potential route. A. P. Hill removed his coat, pulled his sword, and rode with his Light Division as the three brigades drove Banks' men from Cedar Mountain. Confederate losses were low compared to the Federals, 1,307 versus 2,381.[4] Captain John Keely said of the Battle of Cedar Mountain:

> Our movements immediately conformed themselves to those of the enemy, who was next heard of in the vicinity of Cedar Run [Mountain] whither my division was launched with crushing force against him. We charged them through the

---

2 Ibid., 274.

3 *The War of the Rebellion Official Report*, ser. 1, v. 12, pt. 2.

4 Martin Schenck, *Up Came Hill.*

> fields of tall Indian corn, which toppled over on us as we rushed through it, for, the bullets of the enemy literally mowed it down, as they did our ranks, but we rushed fairly over their line of battle completely crushing it by the volume and impetuosity here concentrated.[5]

According to Ray Roddy in his book *The Georgia Volunteer Infantry*, "The 19th lost 19 killed and 116 wounded. The brigade pursued the enemy until nightfall."

The August 21, 1862, edition of the *Atlanta Southern Confederacy* newspaper published a list of casualties suffered by the 19th Georgia at the Battle of Cedar Mountain. The list does not match the number of total casualties cited by Roddy. The list of casualties in the newspaper are as follows:

> Company A—Georgia Volunteers
> 1st Lieutenant W. T. Mead—leg wound
> Private James A. Bane—hip wound
> Private Francis M Hesterly—missing
>
> Company B—Jackson Guards
> Corporal Henry Workman—wounded in the foot
>
> Company C—Palmetto Guards
> 2nd Lieutenant John A. Richardson—groin wound
> Sergeant H. Powell—slight wound in leg
> Corporal W. E. Patman—slight wound in shoulder
> Private Samuel Long—arm wound
> Private Benjamin Dean—arm wound
>
> Company D—Senoia Infantry
> Private Daniel C. Haines—killed

---

5 "The Civil War Diary of Captain John Keely," published in *The Constitution Magazine*, March 15, 1931.

Private A. Conner—leg wound
Private C. T. Digby—leg wound
Private William Persons—wounded in both legs
Private E. M. Woodley—leg wound
Private John A. F. Turnipseed—missing

Company E—Heard County Guards
1st Lieutenant C. J. McDowell—slight wound in thigh
Private W. J. Hearn—slight wound in hand

Company F—Carroll County Guards
Private E. J. Campbell—concussion

Company G—Henry County Guards
Private W. H. Gleaton—killed
Private W. P. Merritt—slight wound in arm
Private J. E. Thompson—slight wound in ankle

Company H—Paulding County Cotton Guards
Sergeant W. T. Medlin—foot wound
Private T. L. Yearwood—knee wound
Private James Ballard—leg wound

Company I—Villa Rica Miners
Private John F. Sampson—killed
1st Lieutenant T. J. Abercombie—slight shoulder wound
Sergeant J. H. Velvin—breast wound
Sergeant W. A. Cheeves—shoulder wound

Company K—Kingston Volunteers
1st Lieutenant Issac A. Roe—leg and thigh wound
Private W. A. Gibson—foot wound

This list was submitted to the newspaper by J. N. Williams, Acting Adjutant, 19th Georgia.

After the battle of Cedar Mountain, Generals Lee and Jackson knew the army of Northern Virginia would have to keep the pressure on John Pope if the rebels hoped to defeat the Union Army before McClellan's troops could join in the fight. To accomplish this, the two devised a plan that was both bold and daring. Jackson's division, along with A. P. Hill's Light Division, would march northwest from Jeffersonton to Amissville, northeast to Orleans, and then Salem. At Salem, the division would turn east toward White Plans, and then through the Bull Run Mountains at Thoroughfare Gap, to Haymarket, Gainesville, and then to Manassas Junction.

The goal was to sever John Pope's supply line from Washington, in hopes of drawing Pope north, away from Richmond and then to mount an all-out attack by Jackson and Longstreet before the Union Army could be reunited.

The flank march by Jackson was designed to catch Pope completely off guard. The men were ordered to make as little noise as possible to avoid detection by the Federal troops along the way. The division left Salem in the predawn hours of August 26. The march was long and difficult, and the men of the Light Division looked like they had marched the fifty-plus miles in two days. According to one of the men in Field's brigade in A. P. Hill's division, "There was no mood for speech nor breath to spare if there had been, only the shuffling tramp of the marching feet, the steady rumbling of wheels, the creak and rattle and clank of harness and accoutrements, with occasional orders to 'Close up! Close up, men!'"

Another of Hill's men wrote, "We were in wretched plight, many were barefoot, many more without decent garment on their backs." Regular rations had not been issued in days, and the speed of the march left no time for foraging. The men grabbed what edible morsels they could along the way. For many that meant raw corn and sour green apples. The diet may have sustained half-famished men, but it also played havoc with their gastrointestinal system. Many had bad cases of diarrhea and dysentery.[6]

By 4:00 p.m. on August 26, Jackson and his troops were within five miles of the Orange and Alexandria Railroad and still they had the element of surprise working in their favor.

Jackson knew the larger Union supply depot was at Manassas Junction. He also knew it was likely heavily defended. Jackson decided to move to Bristoe Station and disrupt the rail service there first. Once in position, the Confederates tried to stop the first train but to no avail. The engineer did pass along information that rebels were at the location and on further north and east at Manassas Junction. When the second train approached, the pursuers were better prepared. They placed obstacles on the tracks that they hoped would derail the train. This time, it worked as the engineer pushed the throttle forward, once he was fired on by the rebels. The train's engine hit the obstructions and careened down an embankment. The cars followed and landed one on top of the other. In no time at all, another train came roaring into the station and hit the previous derailed cars. A third train came streaming up the rails, but the engineer realized what was happening, and he quickly reversed his direction all the way back to Warrenton to inform John Pope. With this phase of his mission complete, Jackson turned toward Manassas Junction. He left troops led by Richard Stoddert Ewell at Bristol Station along with three brigades to monitor the approach of the Yankees.

On August 27, A. P. Hill and General William Booth Taliaferro were ordered to join the Confederates already at Manassas Junction. The Union stores and sutler's supplies found at Manassas Junction were a welcome sight to the hungry, shoeless, ragged soldiers in Jackson's corps. One soldier remarked that it was a peculiar sight to see ragged, dirty, worn-out men gorging themselves on caviar, lobster, canned fish, and other items unknown to men from the South. One soldier mentioned a white, flakey substance that resembled grits. He commented that when added to boiling water, it increased in size to the point of running out of the cooking pot.

---

6 John J. Hennessy, *Return to Bull Run*, 106.

Barrels of liquor and vats of wine were also found. General Jackson was not a drinking man and ordered all the alcohol destroyed. Some say more than a few of the soldiers were brought to tears at the sight of that good liquor spilling on the ground. Some reportedly attempted to catch as much as possible in their canteens.

Before A. P. Hill's Light Division could join in the merriment at Manassas Junction, Jackson ordered him to assist Isaac Ridgeway Trimble's division sent to intercept a potential threat spotted on the Orange and Alexandria Railroad. It was a counterattack ordered by Washington authorities on what they suspected was a Confederate calvary raid at Manassas Junction. The troops sent from Washington were from New Jersey, under the command of General George W. Taylor.

Private William F. Fulton, 5th Alabama, Archer's Brigade, provided a firsthand account of the action to neutralize General Taylor and his men:

> Now, as we moved up into the old field encompassing Manassas, looking off toward Washington, we saw a great blue line of men with guns, marching in a line of battle, with the Stars and Stripes floating on the breeze, coming straight toward us. We were drawn up in line to await their coming. Archer's Brigade was here alone; the rest of our division had gone in another direction. As the blue line approached nearer and nearer, the officers of our command were persistent in their orders; "Don't shoot, men. Stand steady and let them come on." And they came briskly on making right for us, and it seemed that they would walk right over us. Our men began to get nervous and would raise their guns, but the officers were sharp in the command not to shoot: "put down your guns, and stand steady."
>
> Just to our rear, on a little elevation, a battery of artillery unlimbered. Who they were or

> where they came from I never knew, but I saw General Jackson sitting on old Sorrel as stiff as a board, with his eyes intent on that blue line. He was right among the cannon, and suddenly every one of those guns blazed away, right over our heads, sending their missiles into that blue line, which by this time was within a stone's throw. As the artillery fired, we raised a yell and made a dash forward, our guns blazing away. That line of Yanks melted away like wax in a blaze of fire, and it became a fox and dog chase for quite a distance. They broke without firing a gun. Archer's men were running at good speed, firing as they ran.

According to the OR in chapter XXIV, number 188, Jackson ordered Hill to have the 19th Georgia pursue the enemy while the rest of the brigade proceeded down the railroad tracks toward Bull Run. In passing a house on the way, many of the Yanks entered and began throwing their guns out the windows as much to say: "We surrender." The officer in command of this body of men was killed by one of the first shots.[7]

After the battle with Taylor's New Jersey troops, the Light Division was allowed to join the other Confederates enjoying the Yankee victuals. General Jackson had hoped to hold Manassas Junction long enough for Longstreet's Division to join in the feast at the expense of the Yankees. He also knew, however, as did Lee and Longstreet, that he was potentially in a very precarious position. He had marched around Pope and got in his rear—between Pope and McClellan—with the Army of the Peninsula gathering in and around Washington. General Jackson was essentially between the two divisions of the Union Army.

---

[7] Editors of Time-Life Books, *Second Manassas (Voices of the Civil War)* (Alexandria, VA), 85–86.

Any initiative by either Union commander could have made things very uncomfortable for Stonewall. With a potential Union threat near Bristol Station from Pope and a perceived threat from Washington, Jackson decided to move about seven miles north of Manassas Junction. He and his troops were in no position to pursue a pitched battle between two divisions of the Union Army. He had his men burn all the supplies they could not carry and then began to march north.

The always secretive Jackson did not share his next destination with his division commanders. Around 9:00 p.m. on August 27, Taliaferro's division was sent north on the Sudley Road. A. P. Hill's division left Manassas Junction about midnight. Instead of sending written orders to Hill, designating his direction from the junction, Jackson sent a guide. The guide mistakenly led the Light Division toward Centreville. The same scenario took place with Ewell's division, left to perform rear guard duty at the junction. All three divisions were marching north, but none knew their destination. General Jackson sent one of his staff officers to redirect Hill and Ewell to the unfinished railroad cut where they would engage the enemy several times, over the next few days. In his book, *Up Came Hill,* Martin Schenck wrote, "The Light Division was about to engage in some of the most savage and bloody fighting of the war."[8]

Taliaferro's men reached a patch of woods in the northwest quadrant of the First Manassas battlefield. After a few hours of sleep near Centerville on the morning of August 28, the men marched on the Warrenton Turnpike, then north on the Groveton Sudley Road. The division formed the left flank of Jackson's line with Maxcy Gregg's South Carolinians at the far-left position of the line. Edward Thomas' Georgian brigade was to the right of Gregg's, and Fields' brigade was to the right of Thomas. Behind Maxcy Gregg was Branch's North Carolinians. To Branch's right was James J. Archer's brigade, and to his right was William Dorsey Pender's brigade.

Branch, Archer, and Pender served in reserve position as the opening shots at Second Manassas were fired. Pope mistakenly

[8] Martin Schenck, *Up Came Hill,* 170.

believed Jackson's men were headed to Centreville. The errant march of A. P. Hill and Richard Ewell earlier may have helped reinforce Pope's reasoning.

When Pope's first troops arrived at Manassas Junction, they found the burned stores of material and supplies. When they arrived at Centreville, they found it unoccupied by any Confederate troops. Stonewall Jackson was doing his part in stalling an engagement with the enemy until Longstreet and the rest of Lee's army was in position. Stonewall was obviously following a strategy for which he is known: "always mystify, mislead, and surprise the enemy." From around 5:00 p.m. on August 28, until about three the next morning, Archer's brigade was ordered to support a Confederate Artillery Battery south of the Groveton Sudley Road.[9]

The battery is believed to have been the 1st Maryland Battery under Captain W. F. Dement. The Union artillery had spotted Captain Dement and opened fire west of Archer's men. The artillery duel lasted about ninety minutes, after which the brigade marched north, back to the railroad cut in the evening, and engaged the enemy until dark, retaining possession of the cut.

General Pope erroneously concluded that General Jackson was retreating and moving west to rejoin the Longstreet and the balance of the Army of Northern Virginia. In reality, Jackson was not retreating, but he was not ready for a fight either. He knew he had to wait for Longstreet's troops to get closer to Manassas Junction before he was ready to attack Pope. Pope became fixated on destroying Jackson and completely ignored Longstreet and his division moving along the same route taken by Jackson to Manassas Junction, just a few days prior.

On August 29, from 3:00 a.m. to 2:00 p.m., Brigadier General Branch moved along the Groveton-Sudley Road to secure Jackson's left wing of the Confederate Army near Manassas-Sudley Road. Archer's brigade was held in reserve at this time while Gregg's South Carolinians fought the Union to a standstill. At 5:00 p.m., Union General Phil Kearny was ordered to hit Jackson's left by Pope. Kearny

---

[9] Information compiled by the Manassas Battlefield Staff.

was a warrior and, despite losing an arm in the Mexican-American war, a fighter. His attack on Maxcy Gregg's five regiments was ferocious. At one point, Gregg is reported to have rallied his men by saying, "Let us die here, my men," and many did. After about eight hours of fighting, the Confederates were running low on ammunition. Gregg had lost about one-third of his brigade. Archer's men were called up to relieve Pender's brigade on Maxcy Gregg's right to join in the attack by Kearny.

The 19th was under the command of Captain F. M. Johnston. Archer was aware of the enemy's position but would not begin the fight until his men were in position. Once the last regiment, the 1st Tennessee, was up, he gave the order to fire. The men sent forth a volley with "great effect" according to Archer in the OR volume XXIV number 700. It was answered with similar ferocity by the 63rd Pennsylvania under the command of Colonel Alexander Hays. The struggle lasted for twenty minutes or more.

Archer's men maintained their position and repulsed the advancing Yankees. It wasn't long before fresh troops from the 2nd brigade came on again at the same location under Colonel Daniel Leasure. Leasure's men rolled over the unfinished railroad cut.

Regiments from Branch's command moved in to support Archer. Archer also received assistance from Major General Jubal Early's brigade of Virginians.

Again, the attack was repulsed. At the time of the third assault, Archer's men were running low on ammunition. The men started throwing rocks at the Yankees, once their ammunition was exhausted. The Yankees were so stunned by the unorthodox attack, they picked them up and hurled them back at the rebels. The Yankees were again driven back with rocks, the bayonet, and the rebel yell. Charles Field was seriously wounded and was replaced by John M. Brockenbrough from the 14th Virginia. Archer had his horse killed from under him. Here is a picture of what the unfinished railroad cut looks like today and a marker showing where Archer's brigade was located.

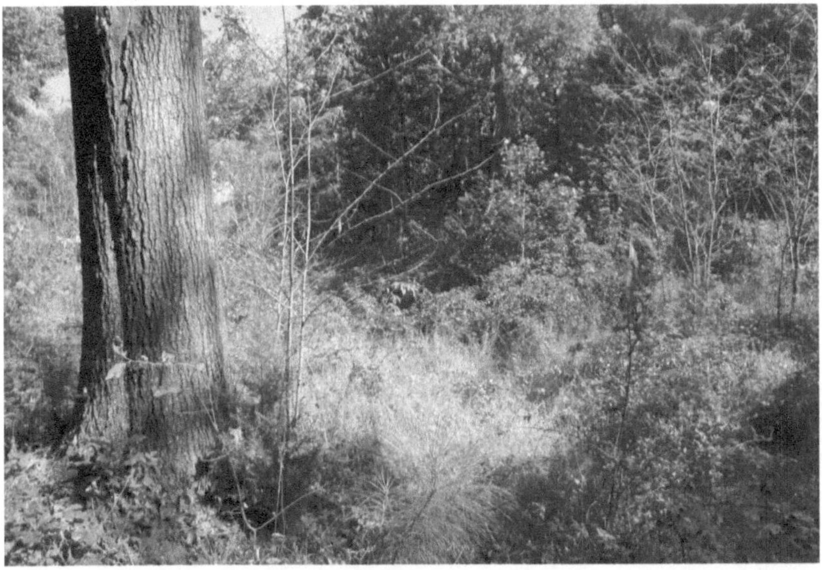

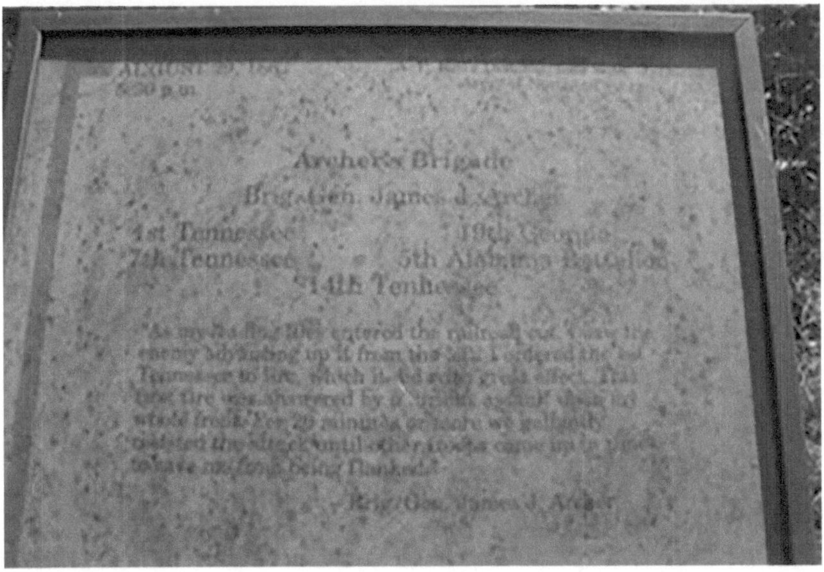

Unfinished Railroad Cut and Archer's Marker at Manassas

From midnight until noon on August 30, Archer's brigade moved east along the Groveton-Sudley Road, then northwest on Catharpin-Sudley Road. The brigade got the opportunity to replenish their ammunition and themselves with much-needed rations.[10]

They returned to the unfinished railroad cut soon after the short respite. The brigade remained in place from around noon on the thirtieth until 3:00 p.m. At 3:45, Brigadier General William E. Starke was in danger of being overrun by Union troops on the far right of the battle line on the west. Archer was sent to assist Starke and ran into Colonel Benjamin C. Christ's Brigade. Archer's men successfully drove the Federals back and pursued them east to the Dogan Farm.

At around 6:00 p.m. Archer was ordered to move four hundred yards west along the unfinished railroad cut to form Jackson's line of advance. Once the advance started, Archer—along with Pender, Pryor, and Featherston's brigades—advanced east to meet the Union troops around the Dogan Farm.

Archer's brigade captured a Union artillery battery belonging to Battery F, 1st Pennsylvania, under Captain Ezra W. Matthews. Just after dark, Archer had his men move east to Matthews Hill, where they found and chased away the 101st New York under Lieutenant Colonel Nelson Gesner. According to Henry M. Garrison from Company D, 19th Georgia, the regiment lay in picket on a hill as the Yankee Army marched east on the Warrington Turnpike, headed to Washington. He said the men could have easily fired on the retreating Yankees, but they had no orders to do so. Garrison wrote he and his comrades had nothing to eat for three days. The next day, the wagons came forward and they had boiled beef, "and I tell you it was good."[11]

---

[10] Manassas Battlefield Staff.

[11] *Reminiscences of the Boys in Gray, 1861–1865.*

The casualties sustained by the 19th as published in the *Savannah Republican* September 23, 1862, are as follows:

Company A
Corporal W. D. Chisholm—wounded in side
Corporal James M. Willis—wounded in shoulder, slightly
Private John J. McCarley—wounded in leg, slightly
Missing: R. Palmer, R. Lemons, and T. C. Selectman

Company B
Captain Dennis S. Myers—wounded in thigh
Lieutenant John McGee—wounded slightly
Sergeant Thomas Ennis—wounded in hand
Corporal Daniel Rogan—wounded in leg
Private James McGee—wounded in head, slightly
Private Timothy Maloney—wounded in leg necessitating amputation
Private Martin N. Nealon—wounded in both thighs
Missing: P. Breen, John Elliott, James Wilson, and Francis Creed

Company C
Private Thomas B. Camp—killed
Private William T. Nixon—killed
Private Satal Thomas—killed
Corporal W. E. Patman—wounded in thigh
Private John M. Edwards—wounded in leg
Private John P. Miller—wounded in leg
Private B. H. Ware—wounded both thighs
Private B. F. Williams—wounded in neck
Private T. F. Rainey—wounded in neck
Private S. F. Floyd—wounded in shoulder, slightly

Private J. Rainey—wounded in breast
Private T. B. Watts—wounded in foot, slightly
Private N. F. Smith—wounded in leg

Company D
Private James Carmichael—killed
Lieutenant W. J. Bridges—wounded in arm
Private James D. Garrison—wounded in right shoulder, right arm rendered useless
Private J. S. Leech—wounded in leg
Private John S. Falls—wounded in arm
Private J. R. Tarpley—wounded in arm, slightly
Missing: A. O. Gay

Company E
Sergeant J. W. Howell—wounded mortally, since died
Sergeant Peter W. Wood—wounded in both legs
Color Corporal William J. Y. Wood—wounded in leg, slightly; promoted to sergeant on the field for bravery
Private W. J. Hearne—wounded in thighs, slightly
Private Eli Upton—wounded in ankle
Private J. C. W. Mercer—wounded in leg
Private W. J. Willoughby—wounded in thigh
Private John B. Samples—wounded in leg, slightly
Private Rufus Samples—wounded in breast
Private G. W. Townsend—wounded in back
Private J. M. Singleton—wounded in hand

Company F
Sergeant W. W. Tomme—killed
Private T. J. Merrill—wounded in thigh, since amputated
Private S. W. Millican—wounded in left shoulder
Private M. J. Reed—wounded in leg, slightly

Company G
Corporal Sidney H. Smith—wounded in hand
Private W. H. Whitaker—wounded in knee, slightly
Private W. J. Allums—wounded in groin, slightly
Private S. M. Oglesby—wounded in groin
Private W. R. Johnson—wounded in shoulder, slightly
Private W. F. Mobley—wounded in chin, slightly
Missing: Elijah A. Rowden

Company H
Private J. J. Roberts—wound in thigh
Private H. C. Adair—wounded in leg
Private J. C. Cheek—wounded in thigh
Private H. J. Turner—wounded in shoulder, slightly

Company I
Lieutenant Francis A. Wylds—killed
Private Thomas J. Mann—wound in leg
Private James A. McVickers—wounded in leg
Private William Hewitt—wounded in thigh, slightly
Private Joel Wood—wounded in leg
Private William E. Fullbright—wounded in shoulder, slightly
Missing: Herman Waldrup

Company K
Lieutenant R. C. Hooper—leg broken
Private Thomas S. Kitchens—wounded in thigh
Private W. J. Freeman—wounded in side
Private W. B. Dye—wounded in breast
Private W. H. Gibbs—wounded in side
Private G. M. Moulden—wounded in head
Private J. B. Wood—wounded in shoulder, slightly

> Private J. M. Taylor—wounded in thigh
> Private James Taylor—wounded in head
> Missing: John Williams, J. L. Roe, W. J. Boyce, and A. K. Scott
>
> The 19th is now attached to "Stonewall" Jackson's army corps, A. P. Hill's Division, Archers Brigade; marched day and night from Orange Court House to Manassas (via Throughfare Gap), whipped the enemy at Manassas, and Burned and destroyed millions of dollars worth of United States stores at that place.[12]

Captain John Keely in Company B of the 19th kept a diary of his activities in the war. The diary was published in the *Atlanta Constitution Magazine*, dated March 15, 1931, and appeared in three installments through April 5. His account of the action at Second Manassas did not include much detail. He said after the battle, he was sent to command a detachment of prisoners detailed to bury the dead. Of the ordeal, he said, "It was the most disgusting and in every way unpleasant duty I had ever been called upon to execute."[13]

John Anderson Richardson in Company C penned a manuscript for a reunion in August 1912. In the manuscript, he detailed actions and the fate of some of his comrades. The manuscript is in the private collection held at the Atlanta History Center, file number MSS 2657. In his document, he mentioned Joseph T. Weaver of Company C from Campbell County, Georgia, now part of South Fulton County. The day after the battle of Second Manassas, Joe Weaver was the only private fit for service in the company. He tells of Sergeant Powell, the only officer fit for duty in company C, running Private Weaver through the drills with the rest of the 19th Georgia, just as if he were commanding a full company. He would say, "Fall in, Joe" and then give the usual command, "Right Dress."

---

[12] *The Savannah Republican*, September 23, 1862.
[13] *Atlanta Constitution Magazine*, 1931.

CHAPTER 5

Lee Moves North

The next day, after the battle of Second Manassas, General Jackson's troops were ordered to move north in an effort to go around the right flank of Pope's retreating army. General A. P. Hill's Light Division was in the lead position as they once again attempted to carry out a flanking maneuver to keep the Yankees from reaching the safety of the heavily fortified capital of Washington. Given the success of the strategy used to flank the enemy at Manassas, the decision was a sound one.

The weather, however, turned, and the rains fell. From many accounts, the thunderstorm was not a small one, and the boom of the thunder competed with the coming blasts of the artillery. Both sources of the ear-jarring sounds had the same effect on the rain-drenched troops. The only difference is that one had the potential to be more deadly than the other.

Rain-soaked roads trod upon by fifteen thousand troops, wagons, and horses made the march difficult at best. General A. P. Hill was criticized by General Jackson for marching at too slow a pace before Manassas—slowed then because of the excessive heat. This time, Hill was determined not to evoke the same criticism from Stonewall Jackson. This time, however, Jackson chastised Hill for moving too fast, thereby, creating large numbers of stragglers in the ranks.

The next day, September 1, General Jackson had his division up and moving by 7:00 a.m. with the Old Stonewall Brigade in the lead. He also sent J. E. B. Stuart's cavalry on a reconnaissance mission to determine the enemy strength near Ox Hill or Chantilly as the battle was known in the north. It should be noted the Union Army typically named battles for major landmarks near the battle site. The Confederate Army usually referred to battles by the name of the nearest town or community. Ox Hill is one exception to this practice, and there are a few others as well.

Stuart's cavalry made contact with Pope's right flank. He returned to Jackson with the news. Jackson then sent A. P. Hill's Light Division south from the Little River Turnpike to feel for the enemy.

General Hill ordered General Branch and Colonel Charles Field to march their regiments forward. The 19th was not engaged in the battle of Ox Hill. In fact, Archer's and Gregg's brigades were never called up to participate in the battle. The reason the two brigades were not called up is lost to history. There is a reference made to the reduction in troops available for duty following the battle of Second Manassas.

The battle of Ox Hill was noteworthy for two reasons: it was one of the rare occasions where the bayonet and hand-to-hand combat ensued, and the one-armed Union veteran General Philip Kearny was killed. In the rain and the confusion of battle, General Kearny mistakenly—this was not his first time of doing so—rode into Confederate lines. The 49th Georgia under Edward Thomas in A. P. Hill's Division realized the rider was a Union officer. They demanded his surrender, which was promptly ignored. As Kearny wheeled around to make an escape, he was shot and fell from his horse immediately. When the officers nearby realized that it was General Kearny, they sent word to Pope and asked to return his body to the Yankees. General Kearny was a warrior and respected by both sides.

Ox Hill was not a decisive battle for either army. After the battle, General Lee resolved to move the army north to Maryland. He sent President Davis a telegram suggesting the same all the while sending his men to the north. Lee's decision to move and the direction to move was almost out of necessity. The war-torn area in northern Virginia could no longer support his army. Foraging for food for troops and fodder for the animals was becoming increasingly difficult. Lee believed the opportunity to feed his army was greater in the untouched fields and orchards to the north.

On September 4, 1862, the 19th Georgia resumed the march from Chantilly to Leesburg. On the September 6, they and the rest of the Army of Northern Virginia crossed the Potomac into Maryland. It should be noted some of the soldiers were reluctant to cross the river into Maryland. Their belief was that the reason they were fighting a terrible Civil War was because the North invaded the South. They did not believe it was right for Southern troops to venture into states outside the Confederacy.

In reality, General Lee had several good reasons for taking the war north: (1) the need for food for men and livestock; (2) he thought he might garner foreign support for the Confederacy with a victory on northern soil; (3) he could take the action further from Richmond; and (4) he believed he could recruit Marylanders to join the Confederacy. It seemed like a valid strategy given the recent string of victories won by the army of Northern Virginia. Some say Lee may have begun to think his army was invincible. The victories, however, came at a high cost.

Unfortunately for Lee, the Southern sympathizers were in eastern Maryland. Instead of the citizenry seeing the Confederates as liberators, Lee's soldiers were cursed and seen as invaders. In the book *Reminiscences of the Boys in Gray*, Henry M. Garrison of Company D, 19th Georgia, recalled a story of a Tennessee Regiment being spit on by two women at Milltown along the march.[1]

The troops were mostly jubilant as they sloshed through the waters of the Potomac. It has been said that even the stoic General Jackson was in a much more agreeable mood as he pushed his men north. The 19th reached Frederick City, Maryland, on September 7.[2]

The rebels left an impression on the citizen of Frederick City, though it was not always a positive impression. One of the residents

---

1 *Reminiscences of the Boys in Gray.*

2 "The Maryland Campaign Major James H. Neal, 19th Georgia," *The War of the Rebellion,* ser. 1, v. 19, pt. 1, Reports Chapter XXXI.

commented that he could smell the Southerners before he could see them. That is probably quite accurate. These men had been on the move and fighting since May in sometimes brutal heat. The scarcity of rations led to foraging and the most plentiful forage diet consisted of corn and apples. A steady diet of raw corn and apples wreaked havoc on the stomachs of the Southern troops. Many of the men suffered from diarrhea from their meager subsistence.

In addition, the dust kicked up by thousands of feet, some shod, some not, as well as wagons and livestock, was sometimes almost suffocating. These men wore the elements as a testament to the journey they had trod. Some of the residents recorded their impressions of the invaders. In *Landscape Turned Red: The Battle of Antietam*, Stephen W. Sears provided a few examples. One resident stated "uniforms were in rags and tatters, faces were unshaven, unkept hair stuck through torn slouch hats and dusty roads added a new layer of dirt. In many regiments the barefooted seemed to outnumber those with shoes."[3]

"They were the dirtiest men I ever saw," said one civilian, "a most ragged, lean, and hungry set of wolves." It is interesting that one resident commented how cheerful the army was, stating most men had a broad grin on their faces.

The stay in Frederick was brief. General Lee had a plan, and he was determined to see it put into action. The details of his plan were recorded for his subordinates on a document known as Order 191. On September 9, Lee's adjunct, R. H. Chilton, was busy making copies of the order to distribute to the generals. General Jackson was to take his division and march to Boonsboro, then Williamsburg, recross the Potomac, and then march to Martinsburg. His objective was the Federal garrison at Harper's Ferry. The Federals there were seen as a possible threat in the event the army had to retreat back to Virginia. Order 191 included the details of Lee's plan to split his army in two. General Jackson would lead his division to neutralize Harper's Ferry, and Longstreet was to march to Hagerstown, Maryland.

[3] Stephen W. Sears, *Landscape Turned Red*, 83.

Harper's Ferry sits at the convergence of the Shenandoah and Potomac Rivers. The town is surrounded by high ground from the Blue Ridge Mountains. To the south is Loudoun Heights, to be taken by General John Walker's two brigades. Lafayette McLaws was to take the high ground north of Harper's Ferry, known as Maryland Heights, and General Jackson was to come in from the west to take command of Bolivar Heights. With Jackson having to swing his division around to approach Harper's Ferry from the west, he had the longest march from Frederick. At Martinsburg, Jackson's troops met some resistance from one squad of Federals. The enemy was driven back to Harper's Ferry without much effort. During the two days the 19th remained on Bolivar Heights, they were "under a tolerably heavy fire from the artillery of the enemy."[4]

According to Major Neal's official report, the regiment had four casualties from the artillery fire. The crest of the hill where the men were positioned afforded modest protection for the shelling. One man was killed and three wounded.

Captain John Keely of Company C, 19th Georgia, recounted the trip to Harper's Ferry in an article written for the *Atlanta Constitution* in 1931. According to Keely:

> We now on a lovely September morning folded our tents like the Arabs, and silently moved away, taking up a line of march towards the enemy, whom we next struck at Harper's Ferry, after having marched 300 miles ten days, barefoot, the vermin crawling over us, and on half rations, for I assure you Jackson's corps knew nothing of the luxuries and seldom anything the comforts to which soldiers generally were used.[5]

---

4 "The Maryland Campaign. As reported by Major James H. Neal, 19th Georgia," *The War of the Rebellion*, ser. 1, v. 19, pt. 1, Reports Chapter XXXI.

5 *Atlanta Constitution*, March 15, 1931.

Captain Keely referred to the surrender of the Union garrison at Harper's Ferry, about twelve thousand troops, as the "proudest moment of his life." The men were jubilant about the supplies, including food, clothes, ordinance, munitions of all types captured with the surrender of the Union troops. The half-naked, shoeless men replenished their wardrobes and filled empty stomachs, complements of the US government. General Jackson left A. P. Hill's division at Harper's Ferry to process the prisoners and captured supplies while he and the rest of his men headed for Sharpsburg, Maryland.

Brigadier General Archer, in his official report, described the march from Harper's Ferry to Sharpsburg as a "long and fatiguing march; many of the men fell, exhausted from the march, by the way, so that when the four regiments of my brigade reached the battlefield, there were only 350 men." Archer was too ill to command the troops on the march, so he turned the command over to Colonel Peter Turney from the First Tennessee.

Archer rode along behind in an ambulance. The Fifth Alabama was left behind at Harper's Ferry. The four regiments of the brigade on the march to Sharpsburg under Archer (now Turney) were the 1st, 7th, and 14th Tennessee, and the 19th Georgia.

Little Mac, George McClellan, was once again given command of the Union Army after John Pope's defeat at Second Manassas. When the Yankees entered Frederick, Maryland, after the rebels left to carry out Lee's Special Order 191, the 27th Indiana was assigned a meadow where the Confederates had bivouacked. Sergeant John Bloss and Corporal Barton W. Mitchell from Company F spotted an envelope in some tall grass. Inside the bulky envelope, the men found a piece of paper wrapped around three cigars. Upon further examination of the find, the men read, "Headquarters Army of Northern Virginia, Special Orders, No. 191." It was signed "R. H. Chilton, Assist, Adj-Gen." Once the document was presented to George McClellan, after several days of indecision on his next move, he shouted, "Now I know what to do!"

The engagement known as Sharpsburg in the South and Antietam in the North was to be the bloodiest single day of the war. General Lee tried to hold on long enough to get his army back to

Northern Virginia. McClellan desired to hold on long enough to defeat the rebels. The battle raged, and Antietam Creek ran red from the blood-soaked ground.

McClellan sent a telegram to General Henry Halleck, who was serving as general-in-chief of all the Union forces, in Washington, on September 17 at 1:20 p.m., stating, "We are in the midst of the most terrible battle of the war—perhaps history."[6]

The armies were successfully destroying each other. General Lee sent a courier to Harper's Ferry with orders for General Hill to march to Sharpsburg immediately. Hill had his men on the march in short order at a grueling pace. It has been written that the tip of Hill's sword was bloodied from pushing his men to the battle. The Light Division reached the southern end of the battlefield about 4:00 p.m. General Lee was observing the battle from a knoll near his headquarters. As he stared at the possibility of defeat of his Army of Northern Virginia, he asked Lieutenant John Ramsay, who was observing through a telescope, "What troops are those?"[7]

The lieutenant noticed the Virginia and Confederate flags. Lee knew then it was A. P. Hill who had arrived from Harper's Ferry. The Light Division had covered seventeen miles in less than eight hours. Hill, in his traditional red battle shirt, was pouring his men into the battle precisely where they were needed at the time. Pender and Brockenbrough were sent to the extreme right while Branch, Gregg and Archer were sent to the left. The site was at the point where the Federals were about to flank D. R. Joneses brigade.[8]

According to Martin Schenck's book, *Up Came Hill*, the first brigade to join the fight was Archer's. Schenck noted the men gave a "wild yell" and charged the unprotected flank of the totally surprised enemy. Major Neal, in his official report, stated that his men were exposed to "heavy fire of musketry while charging through a field of standing corn and, across another field, freshly plowed, but succeeded in driving the enemy from behind a stonewall." Neal further

---

6 Stephen W. Sears, *Landscape Turned Red*, 255.

7 Ibid., 285.

8 Martin Schenck, *Up Came Hill*, 199–200.

stated the regiment held its position despite an advance in large force by the enemy to retake it. According to James Archer's official report on the battle, his losses were fifteen killed and ninety wounded. One of the wounded was Captain T. W. Flynt, 19th Georgia.

Captain Flynt's bravery was mentioned in Archer's report. On the marker below is a photo taken from the Union view of the cornfield.

Sharpsburg Marker

The day's events came to a close with the setting of the sun. As darkness covered the carnage that was the Battle of Antietam, the all-too-familiar calls began to ring out. The wounded and dying asking for water or calling the names of family members back home were the sounds the survivors hated the most. The helplessness in the plight of wounded would haunt most men as they tried to rest. The 19th and the rest of the Light Division lay on the field of battle that night and the next night, according to the official report filed by Major General A. P. Hill.

At 1:00 a.m. on September 19, the division was directed by General Lee to silently withdraw and cover the retirement of the army of Northern Virginia. The men crossed the Potomac at around 10:00 a.m., happy to be back on Virginia soil. That night, the division bivouacked about five miles from Shepherdstown.

At six-thirty on the morning of September 20, Hill was directed by General Jackson to push the enemy, who managed to cross the river in pursuit of the fleeing rebels, back across the Potomac. Near Boteler's Ford Hill, two lines of battle formed. The first consisted of Pender, Gregg, and Thomas under the command of General Gregg. The second line included Lane, Archer, and Brockenbrough, under the command of Archer.

The Yankees had managed to land some artillery pieces on the hills, supporting the infantry. In his official report, A. P. Hill mentioned seventy pieces of artillery amassed by the enemy. As the advance by the Light Division got underway, Gregg was able to brush the enemy aside with modest effort. Pender, however, became "hotly engaged." In Hill's report, he stated the artillery fire was the most tremendous he had ever seen. Archer was informed by Pender of his struggle. In response, Archer moved by the left flank. Once Archer was in place on Pender's left, the report stated a daring charge was made, and the enemy driven back into the river A most terrible slaughter followed, though reports of casualties varied widely.

The rebels fired on the Yankees struggling to recross the Potomac. Witnesses said the river was full of blue-clad bodies floating lifeless on the surface. According to Powell Hill, the Yankees lost three thousand men—killed and drowned—from one brigade alone. In addition, the rebels captured about two hundred prisoners. According to Judge Martin Schenck, A. P. Hill "made what may be his most exaggerated claim of the war." The regiment that successfully crossed the river was the 118th Pennsylvania. In the regimental report, losses totaled about three hundred men. Why Hill's report contained such an erroneous number of enemy casualties is not known.

CHAPTER 6

Back to Virginia

Following the Battle of Shepherdstown, A. P. Hill's division continued to move south to Bunker Hill. The camp was on the Opequon Creek, twelve miles north of Winchester, Virginia. Later in October, the division was ordered to march to Berryville, east of Winchester, nearer to the Shenandoah River. Once in Berryville, the Light Division had orders to destroy the Baltimore and Ohio Railroad. Hill's troops learned the Federals controlled Snicker's Gap, a mountain pass in the Blue Ridge Mountains. West of Snicker's Gap on the western bank of the Shenandoah River was Castleman's Ferry.

The Light Division was charged with picket duty at the ferry, and on November 2–3, Archer and Thomas shared picket duty. According to a member of the 35th Georgia in Thomas' brigade, the enemy occasionally fired artillery shells at the pickets. The pickets had the support of Pegram's and Latham's batteries, but the distance made any thoughts of returning the fire futile. On November 3, the enemy made an attempt to cross the Shenandoah River. According to A. P. Hill's official report dated February 25, 1863, the enemy "were handsomely repulsed by the 19th Georgia and the batteries, with a loss of 200 men."

According to Captain John Keely of Company B, 19th Georgia, the regiment stayed at Bunker Hill for about three months. Keely noted the trek to Fredericksburg started on the last day of November. The division had to cross the Blue Ridge Mountains in the march.

Snow covered the ground as the men, some with shoes and some without, began the trip over the mountains.

One particular day, Captain Keely observed the trailing troops as he reached the summit of one of the many peaks they had to cross. With bands playing and flags flying in the breeze, Keely commented on what an awe-inspiring sight it is to see the men marching in cadence step with bayonets fixed. His view from the summit of the line of marchers zigzagging up the mountain looked to him like a giant serpent slithering up the mountain—the wagon trains with supplies and ambulances "altogether making the most enchanting scene I ever witnessed."[1]

According to Henry M. Garrison from Haralson, Georgia, in Company D, 19th Georgia, the regiment marched about one hundred miles to near Fredericksburg. He further stated in the book *Reminiscences of the Boys in Gray, 1861–1865*, "By the time they reached Fredericksburg the regiment had dwindled down to about 200 men."

The Light Division reached the camps near Fredericksburg on December 11. On the twelfth, the division left the Thomas Yerby estate, Belvoir, at 6:30 a.m. On December 13, Archer's brigade was shown its place in the line of battle on Prospect Hill. The Battle of Fredericksburg began on December 13, 1862, and was actually fought on two different fronts. Jackson's division held a position south of the city know as Prospect Hill, while Longstreet's division was stationed west of the city on Marye's Heights. Longstreet held a formidable defense ensconced behind a stone wall facing open ground with the city further east on the river.

Jackson's troops, on the other hand, had to dig earthworks in its defensive position on Prospect Hill. At the bottom of the hill was the Richmond Fredericksburg and Potomac Railroad. The railroad bed ran generally in a north-south direction, arcing slightly west and parallel to the Rappahanock. Jackson's line somewhat mirrored the railroad running generally northwest. The troops arrived at Prospect

---

1 *Atlanta Constitution Magazine*, March 15, 1931, Civil War Diary Relates Record of Famous Atlanta Company.

Hill and anchored the southernmost or far right of the line. His brigades, in order, consisted of Brokenbrough, Archer, Maxcy Gregg, Lane, and Pender.

Brokenbrough's troops straddled the railroad as it took a southern turn near Hamilton's Crossing. Archer's brigade was stationed on the western side of the railroad, about seventy yards from the tracks. To Archer's left and rear was Maxcy Gregg's brigade of South Carolinians, considered to be in a semireserve position. Much further up the line was Lane's. The six-hundred-yard patch of ground between Archer and Lane was considered too swampy and wooded for the Federals to mount a successful attack. Pender's brigade was placed to the left of Lane's, and Thomas was to Pender's rear. On the right of Thomas was Gregg. All three brigades served as the second line of defense.

Further in a northwest direction were the divisions of Hood, Lafayette McLaws, Robert Ransom, and George T. Anderson. The troops made preparations for the coming battle as best they could, clearing fields of fire, adding more trenches and strategically placing artillery. The men could see in the flats below them the assembling Union soldiers of divisions headed by General George Gordon Meade and General John Gibbon.

The Confederate troops watched in awe as nearly eight thousand men prepared to march against them. One Tennessee solider commented, "Oh! It looked awful and yet beautiful, for it was the grandest sight I ever beheld."

Another Confederate soldier commented that he felt sorry for the Yankees about to march into the "jaws of death." The gap between Archer and Lane was reviewed by A. P. Hill, General Jackson, and General Lee. All three believed the wetlands could not be covered efficiently by an attacking brigade or division. Maxcy Gregg's presence behind the gap added additional confidence that the Federals could not breach the line.

The battle began like most during the war with an artillery duel. The shells were coming and going fast and furious. Artillery was used more for the confusion and demoralizing effect it had on the infantry, rather than an efficient killing technique, although artillery could deal death if used appropriately. Major John Pelham's artillery opened on an entire wing of the Federals and kept them busy for more than an hour. His performance earned him the praise of Robert E. Lee, who referred to him as that "Gallant Pelham."

The Union artillerists were dealing their own brand of confusion and demoralization. At one point, Archer's men abandoned the railroad bed and retreated to the woods behind them. The ferocity of the duel served to unnerve even a veteran. The ground was plowed up, and trees took a lashing. Many of the Union shells overshot the front and landed further back, where the artillery horses and ammunition chests were gathered. So many horses were killed in the duel, the site became known as "dead horse hill." One of the lieutenants in the 19th Georgia tried to comfort his company by saying that artillery barrage was nothing compared to what was to come. He knew instinctively that battle was going to get worse before it got better. His comments did not rank very high on the encouragement scale.

What ultimately inspired the men to go back to the earthworks near the railroad was the presence of General Archer and General Jackson. Amid the torrent of artillery fire, the two rode in various parts of the line, encouraging the men to hold their positions. Archer was known as the "little gamecock" for his relative ease under fire. The men returned to their earthworks and became rather complacent about the shells bursting all around them. One of the Union shells eventually hit one of the ammunition chests and exploded with great effect. This was near the time when the infantry knew they would be called into action.

Jackson had ordered the men to hold their fire until the Yankees got much closer to the line. Archer's men lay in the trenches and picked out a target mark. When the enemy got to their mark, they would open fire. As Meade's Pennsylvanians came on, firing along the way, Archer's men remained silent. Once the Federals reached the railroad cut, Archer shouted the command to fire. A burst of musketry came forth that stunned the Yankees and sent them in as state of confusion. A member of the 7th Tennessee stated, "The work of death began."[2]

---

2 Ibid., 168.

So effective was the firing that the men even stood up and fired at the oncoming enemy. Some of the men in Archer's brigade recalled, after the battle, the enemy were falling like "hay before the mower." Another said, "They [the enemy] melted away like the mist before the morning sun."

The 11th Pennsylvania fell back and regrouped behind the railroad cut. Archer and Lane continued firing at Meade's soldiers with great effect. The men were so focused on the action in their front, they did not realize the gap had been breached by the Keystone Staters. In fact, the Federals impinged on the 19th Georgia in front, flank, and rear.

Colonel Nathan L. Hutchins sent a courier to Archer to let him know the left had been turned. Archer sent a staff officer to ask for help from Maxcy Gregg, not realizing Gregg had been killed and his brigade scattered. The 7th, 11th, and 5th Pennsylvania reserves blasted away at the 19th Georgia. The Georgians began to fire wildly and beat a trail for the woods behind them.

Colonel Hutchins tried to encourage the men to maintain and return fire. Major Neal was wounded but managed to escape with a larger group of men from the regiment.

Lieutenant Evan Woodward jumped in among the men caught in the trenches and asked if they would surrender. The surprised rebels responded, "If you will let us."

Woodward seized the regiment's colors and marched two of the prisoners toward the Union line. All totaled, the Yankees captured about one hundred prisoners from the 19th Georgia. The author's great-great-grandfather, John B. Samples, was one of the men captured.

Samples was wounded in the side and was sent to the rear to be transported to the hospital in Washington DC.

Meanwhile, Woodward, not wanting to leave his present task, gave the 19th colors to a member of the 2nd Pennsylvania reserves to deliver to the division headquarters. Any man who captured a flag from any rebel was awarded the Medal of Honor. The man given the flag, John Schalck, was wounded on the way to the rear and handed the flag off to Jacob Cart of the 7th Pennsylvania reserves to make the delivery. Apparently, Cart made up an elaborate story about how he wrestled the flag away from the color-bearer in a trying struggle. He received the Medal of Honor for something he did not do.

To the right of the 19th, the 14th Tennessee was the next regiment in the line of battle. The Yankees headed straight for this next group of Johnnies in hope of duplicating their success. Before realizing what was taking place on the left flank, many of the Tennesseans saw the escapees from the 19th running to the rear and, not realizing what had happened, cursed the Georgians for abandoning their position. The 14th soon became painfully aware the 19th was surrounded, and the men running to the rear were trying to escape capture. The Pennsylvanians pressed the 14th to the breaking point.

Archer sent another request for reinforcements from Maxcy Gregg. He also pulled the 5th Alabama from the far right to reinforce the crumbling left. The 14th Tennessee met the same fate as the 19th Georgia. The 7th Tennessee, the next regiment to the right, saw the rout and had the same reaction their fellow volunteers had about the Georgians. The 7th Tennessee was running low on ammunition, but the Yankees were as well. The 7th and the 1st Tennessee ran headlong into the attacking foe. Bayonets and clubbed muskets became new tools of death. The rebels held their ground, and the Pennsylvanians began to run out of steam. The 7th and 1st Tennessee contained the breakthrough.

The 5th Alabama headed to the left of the line under orders from Archer. Reinforcements from Early, Hoke, and Atkinson's brigades came forward and helped secure Archer's left. The Yankees fell back to the railroad track and regrouped. Edward Thomas's brigade of Georgians headed for the enemy at the double-quick. The 35th and the 49th regiments caught the brunt of the battle. Despite suffering considerable loss, the men held their ground, repulsing the Federals, not once but four times. The worn-out members of Archer's brigade were sent back to the front at the same time the whole Confederate line lunged forward. The Yankees were stopped, at least on the Prospect Hill front. Further north and west of Fredericksburg, Longstreet's troops inflicted one of the worst defeats suffered by the Union in the war.

As the battlefield action waned, and the sun began to sink to the west, Captain John Keely observed what he called "a scene that was sickening in the extreme." One of the most dreadful times for the soldiers on both sides was after the battle, when the moans and calls for help from the wounded and dying on the field filled their ears. This time, the ghastly ritual was punctuated by fire. The bottom land where most of the battle was fought was covered with sagebrush. Sparks from some of the artillery shells ignited the dry brush.

Wounded men unable to leave the field were seen trying to beat out the flames as they got closer. Some of the men used their ramrods to try to extinguish the flames. Many were burned to ashes as the fire moved across the field. There were a few instances where the fire exploded the cartridge boxes on the wounded, and the shot ripped them to shreds. Help for the wounded could not be given from either side, lest they meet the same fate as those in the field of flame.

Jackson's men slept on their arms in the trenches, expecting the fight to be renewed in the morning. To their surprise, the Federals did not attack the next morning, and the battlefield was mostly quiet, except for the occasional shelling offered by each side. In the darkness of night on December 14, the Federal Army withdrew back across the Rappahannock.

In 1861, the Federal Army refused to meet with the Confederate Army to discuss a prisoner exchange. The Union did not recognize the Confederacy, and any official meeting would signal a departure from their official stance. The problem of what to do with the prisoners was probably the primary motivation to the reconsider the Union policy.

In July 1862, the Union softened its position somewhat when they allowed Union Major General John A. Dix and Confederate Major General D. H. Hill to meet at Haxall's Landing on the James River. The two men were charged with devising a system for the exchange of prisoners. The meeting produced what became known as the Dix-Hill Cartel. The exchange rate in the agreement was based on rank. For example, soldiers of equal rank were exchanged one for one. A corporal and sergeant were worth two privates.

Lieutenants were worth four privates, and the highest-ranking officer, a commanding general, was worth sixty privates.

The able-bodied members of the 19th Georgia taken prisoner at Fredericksburg were exchanged at the end of the month. The captured wounded were sent to Ascension General Hospital in Washington DC for treatment of their wounds. Once healed, the soldiers were sent to Old Capital Prison in Washington. John B. Samples was exchanged in March 29, 1863, at City Point, Virginia. The documents below were taken from the Confederate Service Records.

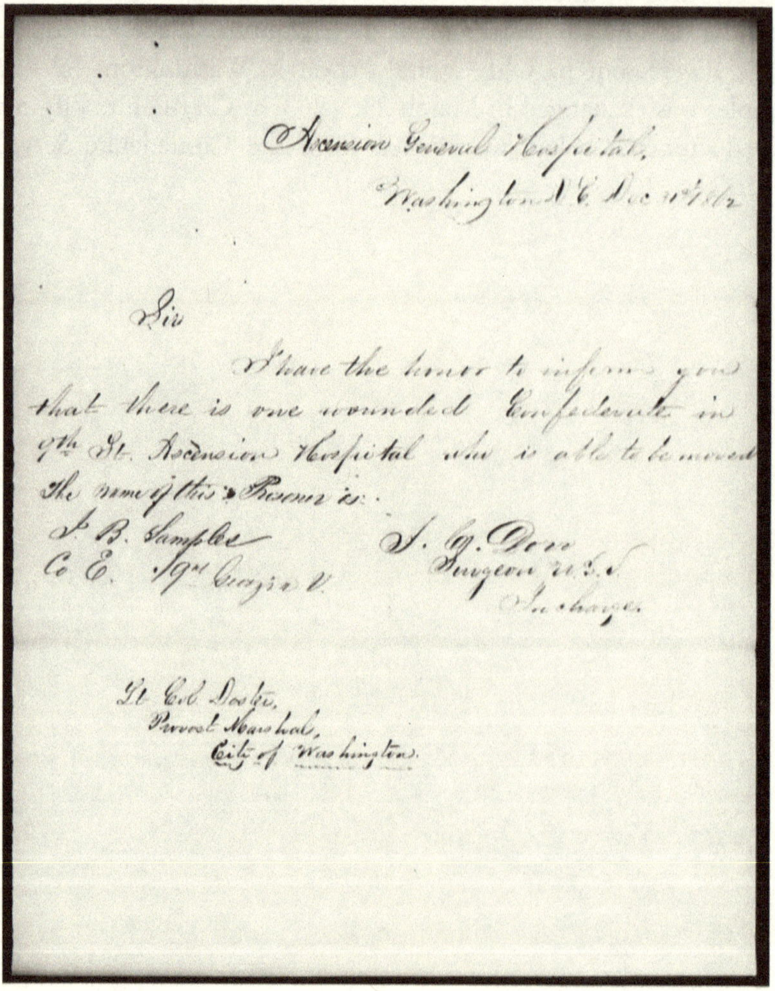

Ascension General Hospital,
Washington D.C. Dec 11th /62

Sir

I have the honor to inform you that there is one wounded Confederate in 9th St. Ascension Hospital who is able to be moved the name of this Prisoner is:

J. B. Samples
Co E. 19th Georgia V.

J. Q. Dove
Surgeon U.S.
In charge

Lt Col Doster,
Provost Marshal,
City of Washington

John B. Samples Hospital Record

CHAPTER 7

Realignment

After Fredericksburg, the 19th Georgia and most of the Army of Northern Virginia went into winter camp around the vicinity of the December battlefield. Early in 1863, the 19th Georgia was reassigned from Archer's brigade in A. P. Hill's division to General Alfred H. Colquitt's brigade in Robert E. Rodes' division.

No official reason for the realignment has survived. Henry M. Garrison from Company D, 19th Georgia, said orders were received to put state troops together as much as possible.[1]

The regiment remained with General Colquitt until the end of the war. The brigade included the 6th Georgia, 19th Georgia, 23rd Georgia, 27th Georgia, and the 28th Georgia regiments. In the winter of 1863, General Lee needed supplies for man and beast. He sent Longstreet's division south to forage for supplies.

Lee's motivation was twofold. He desperately needed food for the winter months, and by sending one division south to look for supplies, he hoped to conserve the rations he had on hand. The railroad track between Richmond and Hamilton's Crossing was in terrible shape. At best, Lee could expect to receive two trainloads of supplies per day. The livestock alone required ninety tons of hay and 107 tons of corn per day to keep them nourished.[2]

---

1 *Reminiscences of the Boys in Gray, 1861–1865*, 255.

2 Stephen Sears, *Chancellorsville*, 33.

The two trains per day could not keep up with the needs of the troops or the livestock. In January 1863, the Army of Northern Virginia numbered ninety-one thousand troops. By late January, the men had their rations cut to four ounces of bacon and eighteen ounces of flour per day. A member of Phillips Legion from Georgia, Sergeant W. R. Montgomery, made the following statement, "The Yankees say that we have a new general in command of our army and say his name is general starvation, and I think for once they are about right."[3]

The men got creative trying to survive the cold Virginia with very little food. The invented a dish called "cush." The full list of ingredients varied depending on what food stuffs were available at the time. It consisted mainly of bacon grease and water with a few edible greens and beef, if available. It cooked down to something similar to hash, mostly without the meat. Another favorite was dough made with flour and water, fried in bacon grease until brown. If bacon grease was not available, the men wrapped the dough around the ramrod and cooked it over the open fire. They found ways to supplement their rations as much as possible with rabbits or even snowbirds. The snowbirds became known as "Confederate gobblers."

After the Union defeat at Fredericksburg, President Lincoln had no alternative but to make another leadership change. This time, he selected Major General F. Joseph Hooker to lead the Army of the Potomac. Hooker did much to improve the morale of the Yankee troops, which was very low after the Battle of Fredericksburg. As Hooker settled into his new role, the two armies were satisfied to keep an eye on each other until spring. General Lee occupied himself trying to anticipate Hooker's intentions, and General Hooker looked for a way to get at the Army of Northern Virginia. Both armies resorted to espionage in an effort to gather information about movements and troop strength.

Hooker devised a plan to send the Union Army west, along the northern bank of the Rappahannock, in an attempt to flank the Confederate left. Extreme care was taken to hide the movement from

3 Ibid., 36.

General Lee. Hooker even had his signal corps send bogus signals to confuse the Confederates about his intentions. He made feints and deceptive demonstrations further south on the river, in hopes of concealing his master plan to flank the rebels. Hooker's hopes were high, morale was good, and he expected to attack Lee before General Longstreet's division could rejoin the Army of Northern Virginia from its foraging mission further south.

Hooker sent Generals Oliver Otis Howard, Henry Warner Slocum, and George Meade to the Kelly's Ford crossing of the Rappahannock beginning on April 27. The Yankees pushed the rebel defenders aside and crossed the river. Once across, Meade was sent to the left to cross the Rapidan River at Ely's Ford while Howard and Slocum continued south to the Germanna Ford crossing. Rain turned the muddy roads turned to quagmires, making movement difficult for men and animals. Once across the Rapidan, Howard moved his division to the far right, facing southwest of the Chancellorsville crossroads. To his left was Slocum's division, and further left was General Meade's division.

General Lee finally discerned the greatest threat from Hooker appeared to be further west. He immediately called for General Jackson to take the Second Corps, consisting of A. P. Hill, Robert Rodes, and Raleigh Colston's divisions, west. William Barksdale's Mississippians and Jubal Early's regiment remained in Fredericksburg to guard the city. The men of the Second Corps were ordered to cook two days rations and be ready to move out in the morning. The march would be in somewhat of a southern arc down the Orange Plank Road to Catharine Furnace, then north to Hazel Grove to near Wilderness Tavern, only about five miles from the Chancellorsville Crossroads. When Hooker was made aware of the movement, he assumed the rebels were retreating.

The flanking march was a difficult one according to Captain John Keely of the 19th Georgia, who referred to it as "severe." Captain Keely, along with the rest of Alfred Colquitt's brigade, led the way as the lead column in Robert Rodes' division. It began May 2, 1863, at seven in the morning. General Lee was waiting to watch his 29,400 men turn south off the Orange Plank Road. The men passing by got an opportunity to see General Lee and General Jackson together, one last time, as Jackson joined General Lee in watching the procession.

The pace was at about two miles per hour with a ten-minute rest every hour. There was one stop along the route, where the marching troops were potentially visible by the Yankees. There was no music, no cheering, no orders being yelled to the men. The march was to be as quiet as possible, so as not to alert the Yankees of the movement. Dan Sickles' men could see rebels moving along the road near Hazel Grove. He ordered the New Jersey Light Artillery to open up on the marchers.

General Jackson ordered General Rodes to have the 23rd Georgia guard the passage. According to Steven W. Sears, the shelling was annoying but did not result in any casualties in the troops on the move. The Confederate march continued to the right flank of the Union Army.

The 23rd Georgia remained around Catharine Furnace until the train of men and munitions wagons had passed. The longer the regiment stayed, the more attention they attracted from the Yankees.

More and more troops were sent to the site, including Hiram Berdan's sharpshooters. The men from David Birney's division successfully kept the 23rd pinned down. Colonel Emory F. Best of the 23rd tried to maneuver away from the action and rejoin the march. He had his men retire to an unfinished railroad cut, but the line was short and easily outflanked by the Yankees. Colonel Best lost 296 men to capture by the Federals and had three wounded. The prisoners were marched to the rear.

The leading troops of Rodes's division, Alfred Colquitt, Alfred Iverson, Edward O'Neal, and George Doles reached the Orange Turnpike around 3:00 p.m. Rodes began putting his regiments into position in a line of battle that stretched about three quarters of mile on each side of the road. Colquitt's Georgians were placed on the far right of the line, south of the Orange Turnpike.

Major General Howard, the far right of the Union line, and his men were cooking their evening meal. Rifles were stacked, coffee was simmering, and the men were in a more or less relaxed mood. At 5:30, General Jackson asked General Rodes if he were ready, to which he responded, "Yes, sir." With a nod from Jackson to his bugler, the signal was given up and down the line to move forward through the wilderness. Captain John Keely said the place was appropriately named. He noted the number of scrub timber and the undergrowth that made the movement difficult.

The most westward regiments of the Union Army heard a distant bugle followed by some commotion in the wood line to their right. The next scene was a large number of animals running from the woods, into the open field. Witnesses saw quail flying from treetop to treetop. There were deer, rabbits, and even one reported bear seen running from the wood line. The next sound the Yankees heard had to send a chill down their collective spine.

The rebels let loose with the rebel yell and charged full speed on to Howard's division. Many Yankees described the rebel yell as a sound like no one has ever heard before. It has been said if one hears it, it will raise the hair on the back of one's neck, and if one claims to have heard it without getting that sensation, then one has never heard it.

The men of Howard's division were overrun and thrown into total chaos. Many Yankee prisoners were taken. The battle was a complete rout and, many believe, General Lee's greatest victory.

General Colquitt did not have his best performance at Chancellorsville. He was ordered to advance forward down the south side of the Orange Turnpike. He advanced but then became concerned about being flanked on his right. His brigade was the far right of the Confederate line. Colonel Andrew J. Hutchins of the 19th Georgia mentioned Colquitt's concern about the right flank in his official report, writing:

> I was ordered by him [Colquitt] to detach my command and look after the flanking party. I made a charge to the right, and moved forward a few hundred yards, but did not meet the enemy, but could see them fleeing before me, out of range of my guns. I deemed it useless to proceed any farther in that direction, so I turned to my

> left and followed the brigade. While making to the left, the enemy threw a few shell at my regiment and wounded two of my men. Just before dark, we rejoined the brigade, and were placed an hour or two afterward on the front line, near the batteries on our line, close to the Plank Road.

Colonel Hutchins further stated in the report the regiment slept on their arms that night. With the approaching darkness, Rodes called an end to any further actions at 7:15 p.m. Three of the leading brigades did not get the message from Rodes and continued their forward progress as darkness added to the confusion. Hooker called up the Union Cavalry to help stop the panicked infantry still streaming to the rear. Both Union and Confederate troops became confused and disoriented in the darkness. Men became jumpy at the slightest movement, each anticipating the approach of the enemy.

Stonewall Jackson decided to follow up his earlier success with a night attack. He had a local guide help reconnoiter. He ran into A. P. Hill on the Orange Plank Road who had his men up to relieve Rodes brigade. No one informed Jim Lane in Hill's division that Jackson and other staff officers were in front of their position. The 18th North Carolina believed the sound of galloping horses approaching from the front was Union Cavalry, and his men fired on the approaching riders. Unknowingly, the 18th North Carolina fired on Jackson and his entourage. General Jackson was hit, and several others in the party were killed or wounded severely. A. P. Hill was also wounded but still able to come to the aid of Jackson. Litter bearers were called up as the Union Army began shelling the area.

Jackson was carried to the rear for medical attention but not before being dropped from the litter twice because of intense shelling from the enemy artillery. The loss of Jackson was a terrible blow to the Army of Northern Virginia. His death, a few days later, was mourned throughout the South.

Chancellorsville may have been General Lee's greatest victory, but there he also suffered his greatest loss in General Jackson. The Battle of Chancellorsville claimed 449 troops from Colquitt's brigade. The after-battle report listed nine killed, 128 wounded, and 312 missing. The large number of missing is from the captured members of the 23rd Georgia near Catharine Furnace. The 19th Georgia's loss was three killed, thirty-three wounded, and eleven missing.

CHAPTER 8

Charleston—under Siege: Water, Water Everywhere, and Not a Drop to Drink

Charleston was seen by the Federals as the cradle of the rebellion. As such, the Union Army and the Lincoln administration were determined to punish the city for firing the first shot that started the war and to make the state pay for being the first to secede. The attempt to bombard Charleston into submission lasted almost the duration of the war.

Fort Sumter sat in the middle of the channel that was, in essence, the front door of Charleston. To the northeast of Sumter was Sullivan's Island with Fort Moultrie. To the southwest on James Island was Fort Johnson. Almost due south of Fort Sumter was Morris Island, a long, narrow strip of land that ran nearly in a north-south direction. At the northern point, nearest to Fort Sumter, was Cumming's Point and the location of Battery Gregg. The battery was named for Brigadier General Maxcy Gregg, who was mortally wounded at the Battle of Fredericksburg in December 1862. Further south of Battery Gregg was Battery Wagner, originally known as the Neck Battery. In November 1862, it was renamed Battery Wagner in honor of Lieutenant Colonel Thomas M. Wagner of the 1st South Carolina Artillery who was killed earlier in the conflict.

To call Battery Wagner a fort would be a compliment. According to Captain Keely from Company B of the 19th, the fort "was an immense pile of sand, covering sheds made of heavy logs." The occupants were relatively safe from shelling by the Union navy while inside the battery. Much to the surprise of the Federals, sand could withstand the shelling a little better than brick and mortar forts.

The sand, however, had to be constantly replaced after each shelling by the navy. The repairs took manpower. It was hard, grueling work on the hot, humid South Carolina coast.

The 19th left Wilmington, North Carolina, along with its sister regiment, the 6th Georgia, on July 9, 1863, headed to Charleston. The other two regiments under Colquitt's command, the 27th and 28th Georgia, remained in Wilmington until August 10, 1863.

The 19th reached Fort Johnson on James Island on July 14. Below is a picture of what Fort Johnson looks like today and a view of Fort Sumter from the shore. To the left of Fort Sumter is Sullivan's Island and to the right is the sand marsh before reaching the northern tip of Morris Island.

Picture of building at Fort Johnson

Picture of Fort Sumter from the shore

It wasn't too long after the 19th reach Charleston that the regiment was called into action. A reconnaissance mission ordered by Confederate commander Brigadier General P. G. T. Beauregard revealed the presence of Union troops on the south end of James Island near Grimball's Plantation. The Union forces included the 10th Connecticut and the 54th Massachusetts.

General Johnson Hagood saw an opportunity to pin the Federal troops against the Stono River. On July 16, Brigadier General Alfred Colquitt was ordered to march southward and come behind the Federals to cut off their line of retreat while Hagood pressed from the north. The 10th Connecticut was quickly pushed aside. Colquitt's men soon overran the 54th Massachusetts skirmishers at Rivers' Causeway and pushed them back into the main body of troops.

The 54th Massachusetts was an all-Black regiment, commanded by Colonel Robert Gould Shaw. Shaw had his men drawn up in line of battle. The fire was intense, and the Black troops stood their ground as violent hand-to-hand fighting ensued. The larger Confederate force overwhelmed the 54th Massachusetts, and one company was cut off from the rest of the regiment. The Union warships extracted as many of the troops from the site as possible under fire from the Confederates.

Federal losses were mainly from the 54th Massachusetts. The rebels also gathered a number of prisoners, which presented a new problem for the Confederate leadership: what to do with the Black soldiers? Orders were given that the Black prisoners were to be treated humanely.

The rebels did not always heed the orders. In a letter written to his wife, Sarah, D. D. Morris wrote, "We had to fight niggers here an' I don't like it one bit, but we didn't take no prisoners, only fifteen, and the officers couldn't hardly keep us from killing them they run up to us and try to give up but we would hear them but we would shoot them down."[1]

Prisoners who survived the battle, until further direction could be provided, were housed in the Charleston jail. Garrison duty performed by the soldiers at Battery Warner was dangerous and exhausting. The men inside the battery were holed up in bombproof shelters most of the daylight hours. The men on picket duty outside the battery had to endure the hot South Carolina sun and constant shelling from the enemy. D. D. Morris wrote to his wife, "I was covered up in the sand by the bombshells. They would burst in five feet of me and I thought ever minute I was gone up the spout."

The bombardment from the Federal Navy ships each day removed much of the sand that offered a little protection to the men in the battery. Each night, the sand blown off during the day's shelling had to be replaced. The men spent most of each night in the fort, replacing the sand. According to Captain John Keely, sand "had to be replaced nightly by almost superhuman labors. Every soul had to work, and that hard, for on the reconstruction of the roof depended our safety."[2]

The work was so exhausting, each brigade spent only a few days at the battery, to be replaced by a fresh brigade arriving from James

---

1 Morris Family Letters Georgia Archives Doc—6354, RG-SG-S 48-1-1, Accession 1978-0052 M, MF-230.

2 "Captain John Keely Diary," *Atlanta Constitution Magazine*, March 1931—Atlanta History Center.

Island. The boat ride from James Island to Morris Island was equally dangerous and had to be accomplished under cover of darkness. There is one account of the 19th Georgia not performing their best at garrison duty. The quote in the *Official Record of the War of the Rebellion* is as follows:

> I regret to mention that the Nineteenth Georgia Regiment did not display the high discipline which its brilliant achievements on so many fields in the past warranted me to expect, and that its colonel commanding betrayed too much negligence. As I dislike to interrupt the general harmony of the command, I adopted no stringent measures, and am happy to say that no evil resulted, except the wounding of a few members of this regiment in the commissary house, where they had no business to be, excepting the two on guard.[3]

The 54th Massachusetts made its ill-fated charge on Battery Wagner on July 18, 1863. The attack was brutal and losses of Union troops were heavy. Colonel Shaw and many of his men were killed at point-blank range, attempting to scale the walls of the battery. The 19th Georgia was camped at Fort Johnson, when the much-heralded attack by the 54th Massachusetts took place.

On August 3, 1863, at about 4:00 p.m., some of the men were gathered around an old commissary building in Battery Warner. According to the official record, the men were enjoying a little shade cast by the building structure. Shots were heard from a gunboat. One of the shells hit a post holding up the old building and splintered it, resulting in the death of Private C. McLean of Company K, 19th Georgia, and wounding John Raney, Private J. M. Taylor, and Private

---

[3] OR, Chapter XL, Operations on Morris Island, SC #465.

J. A. Nix, all from the same company. Lieutenant J. R. Elliott of Company G, 19th Georgia, was also wounded by the blast.[4]

In the same report, Surgeon S. P. Johnson of the 19th Georgia became the chief surgeon and, according to the report, proved very efficient. The report further stated that under Johnson's care, the hospital was much improved.

The rebels eventually vacated Morris Island on September 3, 1863. The reason for the departure was the difficult duty required to maintain the battery. There was also the lack of potable water. In a letter to his wife dated August 11, 1863, D. D. Morris wrote, "The water here taste like dead men smell and every time I drink it, I throw up."[5]

After the attack of the 54 Massachusetts, the dead had been entombed in the sand around the battery. It is no wonder the water tasted "like dead men smell."

In a letter written by Willis Pentecost Menefee to his mother, dated September 4, 1863, he wrote, "We had to vacate Morris Island last night we have not got any troops on it at all."[6]

W. P. Menefee, born 1844 in Palmetto, Georgia, was in Company C, 19th Georgia. He was killed at the Battle of Weldon Railroad on August 19, 1864. He is mentioned in a document written by Captain John Anderson Richardson for a 1912 reunion. The captain recalled Menefee was shot "while standing on a breastwork firing at the enemy."

The actual site of the Morris Island fort is no longer visible as erosion and time have taken their toll. The ocean claimed the fort before the end of the 19th century.

The 19th Georgia spent seven long months on the South Carolina coast performing garrison duties and trying to survive the constant shelling by the enemy. The regiment was sent to various locations around the coast as needed, including Forts Sumter, Johnson, and Wagner. This letter written by Darling D. Morris, Company

---

4 Ibid., SC #457.

5 Georgia Archives Document, 6354 Accession 1978-0052 M title MF—230 "Morris Family Papers."

6 Menefee-Timmons Papers, Atlanta History Center.

G, 19th Georgia Regiment to his wife, Sarah, provides a glimpse of some of the difficulties the troops had to endure:

> Camp One James Inlet near Charleston July the 21, 1863
>
> To Mrs. S. E. Morris Dear Wife,
>
> I this morning seat myself to try to write you a few lines to inform you that I am in common health at this time. Hoping my lines may come safe to hand and find all well and doing well.
>
> Sarah, I ain't got nothing interest to write you only we have had some fighting here and the fight is a going on yet and the cannon is firing over us it is hard to seat down and write a letter and the cannon shooting over me all the time but this may be the last.
>
> Sarah, I sent you a letter the morning we landed here and sent you some postage stamps. I don't know whether you got it or not. Tell and to write to me. I have write to them and ain't got no answer from them. Watermelon is worth from two to three dollars here. We are surrounded by water here, and we can't get out only when they have a mind to let us out.
>
> Sarah, if the Yankees whip us here, they will take us all prisoners for we can't get out of here

and if they take me a prisoner, they will take me dead for I don't intend to give up.

So I must come to a close. Yours Truly,
DD Morris[7]

Other insights come from a letter from William H. Johnson to his father:

James Island, South Carolina

November 27, 1863

Dear Father:

Everything in and around Charleston remains in about same condition as when I last wrote except that the shelling has caused a considerable exodus of the noncombatants. The lower front of the city is becoming just, most of the arsenal horses being removed to the front of King Street using. But there is not the confusion and excitement that under the circumstances might reasonably be expected. The danger seems to have been so long anticipated that everyone was furloughed for it. A detachment of Twenty-five (25) men which had been on duty at Sumter for sixteen (16) days returned last night. They were relieved by a detachment from our regiment. We kept our duty staying all the night, fifty (50) men and officers. So far we have been very fortunate indeed, not having had a man killed and but one wounded and he only slightly. From the officer in charge of the detachment I gathered some inter-

[7] Georgia Archives Document, 6354 Accession 1978—0052 title MF—230, "Morris Family Papers."

esting facts of the condition of the old. There remains in the fort still mounted five heavy guns two of which having towards the city. There are also there twelve or fifteen (12 or 15) pieces of light artillery. Nothings which would be very reliable in an assault with barges. Should the enemy succeed in gaining a landing and occupy the fort, it is intended to withdraw the infantry into the bombproofs, and fight them at the sally-fronts (intrenched) where the men could repel five-hundred, also to flank the in rear of the fort in the parapets of the sally-fronts of the fort where they can command the whole of the interiors, while the only approach to them will be strongest the sally-front, which would be certain death, or to scale the sea wall, which would be exceedingly difficult. At the same time they would be exposed to the concentrated fire of our batteries of James and Sullivan Island and of our earthworks while our men would be completely protected.

The garrison consists of three-hundred (300) infantry and sixty-five or seventy (65 or 70) artillery. As you imagine taking Sumter by assault is no child's play. General Beauregard has requested of General Taliaferro commanding this island that the garrison in future be supplied from this brigade and from the 25 SCN and the Charleston Battalion. This request, of course, originated with Major Elliot commanding Fort Sumter. This is quite a complement. Sumter being the host of danger is, of course, the host of honor. But I cannot say that such compliments are fully appreciated by our Brigade.

Eighteen months ago they might have been rather fond of it. But they feel now that they have done quite enough for glory.

The health of the Regiment continues very good. There has been one death in camp since my return, Peter Leatherwood, of my old company. He was in every respect an exemplary soldier, though a private man. He remarked just before death that he had been a bad boy but had fought the Yankees for nearly three years as well as he could, which seemed to be much consolation. Poor fellow, he deserved a better death. It seems rather hard that after fighting bravely so long that he should so tragically die in Hospital instead of in the battle front.

Our regiment is very well clothed except for shoes, which are very scarce. We should get in few days a lot of clothing from the State of Georgia in which there are a number of cloth shoes, much better than no shoes. Bed clothing is also very scarce but the climate being mild we may no doubting make out.[8]

---

8 Official Records of the Confederate Soldiers reports Peter M. Leatherwood died of illness in November 1863.

CHAPTER 9

The Battle of Ocean Pond

During the first two years of the war, Florida was not given much thought by military leaders, north or the south. The thousands of miles of coastline were impossible for either army to adequately defend, given the limited number of troops. In addition, the state's distance from other sites closer to the United States and Confederate capitals kept Florida essentially out of sight and out of mind. The north was satisfied to continue the anaconda plan proposed at the beginning of the war by General Winfield Scott. His plan was simple, but it did require substantial amounts of men and material. Scott believed he could strangle the Confederacy by blockading the ports from Virginia, all the way around Florida, to the coast of Texas. The Federal navy worked continually to stop smugglers from entering Southern ports with much-needed supplies, both military and civilian.

They achieved some success but not complete closure of the ports. One reason was the money to be made by blockade runners. The South was so desperate for even staples like flour and sugar that many entrepreneurs saw an opportunity to make a small fortune. For many, blockade running was lucrative enough to offset the risk.

By the end of 1862, the Federal Navy had some relative success at capturing a foothold in a few areas in Florida. By the end of 1863, Union officials believed there might be a benefit to mounting a land excursion to the interior of the state. Major General Quincy

A. Gillmore was the commander of the Federal Department of the South. He made a compelling argument for the excursion based on achieving the following objectives: exploitation of the state's vast natural resources, cutting off the important supplies sent from the state to the southern army, preventing Confederates from destroying rail lines from Union controlled railroads to repair lines to be used by the Confederacy, and the recruitment of Blacks to serve in the US Colored Troops.

There was also the unrealistic expectation of Federal occupation in key areas successfully folding the state back into the Union. The reunification of Florida back into the Union was seen by Lincoln as an opportunity to improve his chances of success in the 1864 election.

On February 7, 1864, Federal troops landed in Jacksonville with the intentions of accomplishing the enumerated goals. General Truman Seymour had, under his command, the 7th New Hampshire, 7th Connecticut, the 8th US Colored Troops, the 54th Massachusetts, 47th New York, 48th New York, 115th New York, the 2nd South Carolina (Union), and the 3rd US Colored Troops. Mounted troops included the 40th Massachusetts Cavalry and three artillery batteries.

General P. G. T. Beauregard was the Confederate commander of South Carolina, Georgia, and Florida. He was made aware by lookouts stationed near the coast of thirty-five enemy ships taking to the sea. Soon after the Union landing, General Joseph Finegan telegraphed Beauregard about the movement of the enemy.

Before the war, Joseph Finegan was a businessman in Fernandina, Florida. He was born in Clones County, Ireland, on November 17, 1814. He was appointed brigadier general by the Confederate War Department and charged with monitoring enemy actions in northeastern and north central Florida. He immediately requested more troops from Beauregard to defend against the Union threat. General Jeremy Francis Gilmer in Savannah was ordered to send the troops under his command to Florida to aid General Finegan. Beauregard sent Colquitt's brigade to Savannah from Charleston to replace the troops sent to Finegan.

The intentions of the Union were not fully known around Charleston as the siege had turned into a stalemate.

General Finegan estimated the Union strength at between six thousand to seven thousand troops. He had only 1,267 enlisted men and officers, and the troops were not consolidated in one spot. The men were in a number of different locations from the Atlantic coast to the Gulf of Mexico. Finegan's concern over the landing of such a large number of enemy troops was justifiable.

Once landed, General Gillmore took control of Jacksonville and established a perimeter on the western edge of the city. The expedition planned to move west to the interior of the state the next morning. When the troops got underway the next morning, they left in three columns by three different routes, all heading west. The mounted soldiers rode ahead of the infantry, brushing up against small groups of Confederates along the way. Union Colonel Guy Henry had his command in Baldwin, Florida, by 7:00 a.m. on February 9. As the Federals continued to head west, they took a number of prisoners and seized and destroyed and estimated $1,000,000 in Confederate property.

On February 13, the Union force was concentrated around Barber's plantation in northeastern Florida. Seymour was convinced he could take his force all the way to Lake City. There he hoped to destroy or confiscate even more Confederate supplies. Local residents along the way had falsely convinced Seymour of Union support all along. He was possibly driven by the belief the state might be returned to the Union. As Seymour continued west, toward Lake City, Finegan sent an urgent plea to General Beauregard for more troops.

Alfred Colquitt's brigade had been retained around Savannah, Georgia, until Beauregard could determine the intentions of the Federal Army around Charleston. Once Beauregard was satisfied, the movement around Kiawah by Union General Alexander Schimmelfennig was a diversionary move. He ordered Colquitt to move as soon as possible to General Finegan. It is widely believed the arrival of Colquitt's brigade made the difference at Olustee.

On February 14, Colquitt was ordered to move to Florida as soon as possible. Two days later, the 19th Georgia, 27th Georgia, and the 28th Georgia boarded the Florida, Atlantic, and Gulf Coast Railroad, en route to Madison, Florida. The 6th Georgia regiment had been sent to Finegan on February 10. Private Hail of the 27th Georgia wrote in a letter back home to family that the men left Savannah on a Tuesday and that they had two days of hard marching from one railroad to the other.

William Fredrick Penniman from the 4th Georgia Cavalry wrote of the arrival of Colquitt's Brigade:

> The following day trainload after trainload began to arrive, which proved largely to be Colquitt's Georgia Brigade, who were veteran soldiers just from Virginia, where their experience had been brought upon many bloody battle fields, whilst this was to prove our very first experience. I couldn't help but notice the entire brigade seemed to be composed of mere youths, the majority doubtless being under 21 years of age, certainly under 25. They seemed to be such a "devil may care" set as a whole, that to me they were a curiosity, realizing as I did the renown they had already earned as a fighting brigade.[1]

The men reached Station number 9 during the night of February 17 and began marching to Madison, Florida, at sunrise the next day. They were ordered to leave all baggage, except for cooking utensils and whatever they could carry in their knapsack. At sunrise the next day, the men arrived at Madison, about a thirty-mile march in twenty-four hours. It is said that not a single man was left on the side of the road, and there was no straggling along the route.

Once in Madison, the men hopped on the cars and rode to Lake City, Florida, and picked up the 6th Georgia. The men rode on to Olustee Station and disembarked the cars the evening of February 18. The next day, the men had a quiet day of rest. The estimated

[1] Robert P. Broadwater, *The Battle of Olustee, 1864.*

strength of the 19th Georgia at Olustee was 591 men, rank and file. On February 20, General Finegan ordered the 64th Georgia and two companies from the 32nd Georgia to march about three miles east to meet the enemy. Reports had been received that the Yankees were spotted destroying the railroad tracks. Orders were to engage them "lightly" and draw them toward the main Confederate line.

Colquitt received orders to move toward the enemy with the Chatham Artillery and the 23rd Georgia. The remaining regiments were ordered to follow as soon as they could be formed in line to do so. At a crossroads not too far distant, Colquitt met up with the 64th Georgia, and then the Confederate cavalry pursued by the enemy.

Colquitt quickly ordered Gamble's battery to take a position at the Crossroads, and he ordered Colonel John H. Neal to form the 19th Georgia to the right of the guns. The battle began in earnest as both sides became hotly engaged. Colquitt immediately requested reinforcements from Finegan. The 6th Florida Battalion was sent in—under fire—to the right of the 19th Georgia. The first enemy troops to be engaged were the men of the 7th Connecticut. The fire was intense from both sides.

The 64th Georgia was relatively inexperienced, and some of the men began to turn and head to the rear. Had it not been for Colquitt's veterans, the whole brigade might have withered under the repeating rifles used by Union troops.

The Union troops were being sent into the battle piecemeal, which proved fatal to the Yankees. The engagement reached its crescendo near 3:00 p.m. when, according to Captain John Keely, the regiment had expended all its ammunition. The situation became desperate, and he ordered the men to fix bayonets in anticipation of a charge by the enemy. In just a few short moments, additional ammunition reached the near desperate men. Captain Keely said the men grabbed the cartridges like hungry men grab loaves of bread.

Afterward, he said, "There are moments in battle when flesh turns into granite, in fact, the soldier becomes alternately a demon and a statue. This was one of those times."

In an article written for the *Atlanta Constitution Magazine*, Keely recalled the fate of Corporal Sam Clarke, Company C, of the

19th Georgia. Clarke called to Keely, who couldn't understand him over the noise of battle. Keely moved closer to Clarke, who cupped his hand to his mouth to speak in Keely's ear. At that time, Corporal Clarke was hit in the head, scattering his brains all over Keely's face and chest.

Olustee Battlefield

CHAPTER 10

Back to Virginia Again

The 19th Georgia remained in Florida for about two months after the battle of Ocean Pond. Captain Keely mentioned in the article for the *Atlanta Constitution* that he was lying in his tent a few days after the battle, when a soldier cut down a tree too close to his tent. The top of the tree landed on Keely's tent, causing a contusion on his foot. Keely was sent to the hospital in Monticello, Florida, for a couple of weeks to recover. Once healed, he was sent back to the regiment.

When the time to move north arrived, Colquitt marched his men up through a portion of the Okefenokee Swamp. Keely wrote of what a miserable march it was, mostly through ankle and waist-deep water. The roads, if one could call them roads, were nothing more than trails. Keely described the terrain:

> A more horrible place you cannot conceive on earth. A miserable waste covered with stinking stagnant water, from which fever and ague rise in perfect clouds. Studded with pine trees and matted by briars, here and there a patch of dry land appearing.[1]

---

1 *Atlanta Constitution* article, March 15, 1931.

Upon arrival at the first station of the Gulf Railroad, the regiment boarded the cars and headed back to Charleston. The men disembarked and marched back to their old camp on James Island. Before they could drop their gear at the old quarters, the men were about-faced and marched back to the cars. The brigade was ordered back to Virginia in defense of Richmond.

Captain Keely was ordered to take a contingent of the 19th Georgia to occupy Fort Sumter. Keely and his garrison remained at the fort for thirty days. During that time, a "feeble assault" made by the enemy was repulsed, Keely noted.

When Captain Keely and his men rejoined the brigade in Virginia, they were engaged at the battle of Drewry's Bluff. The battle, also known as the Battle of Fort Darling, took place on May 16, 1864. Drewry's Bluff is located on the James River, south of Richmond. The regiment was assigned to Major General Robert F. Hoke's division under the command of General P. G. T. Beauregard. At the (second) battle of Drewry's Bluff in mid-May 1864, Ben Butler's Army of the James was almost destroyed by Beauregard.

General Lee had his hands full with US Grant, north of Richmond. The Overland Campaign begun by Grant in May 1864 brought the opposing armies together at the battles of the Wilderness, Spotsylvania, and Cold Harbor. Lee desperately needed more troops to defend against Grant's continued assault on Lee's right flank. With each engagement, the armies moved further south as Grant worked to outflank Lee on his right.

General Lee was the commanding general of the Army of Northern Virginia. He had no authority to command P. G. T. Beauregard in any action. All he could do was suggest actions to Beauregard. After several days of "suggestions" through President Davis and to Beauregard directly, Lee finally got a commitment to send more troops from south of the James River to the vicinity of Cold Harbor. Robert F. Hoke's division was dispatched to Richmond by rail, arriving on May 31. Once in the capital city, the soldiers commenced a march that took them back to the same areas they fought more than two years prior. They marched through Mechanicsville, Gaines's Mill, and on to Cold Harbor.

It was a slow march. Many of these men were somewhat out of "hard marching" condition. The 19th Georgia, like many of the regiments, had spent about seven months in essentially the same location in South Carolina. During their time in South Carolina, the daily marching earlier in the war had ceased to be part of the daily routine. Hoke's division marched east along the New Cold Harbor Road. Once past New Cold Harbor, the bulk of the division filed off the road to the left.

Colquitt's brigade went left of the road and anchored the far right of the Confederate line. The last of the out of condition troops did not all arrive at Cold Harbor until June 1. They were placed into position replacing cavalry units on the frontlines facing Cold Harbor.

Once in place, the rebels began entrenching and, in a relatively short time, had created a formidable defensive line. The Confederate works ran roughly north to south, east of Gaines's Mill, the site of the June 1862 battle. To Colquitt's left and straddling the New Cold Harbor Road was Hagood's South Carolinians. To Hagood's left was Thomas Lanier Clingman's brigade, and to his left was Wofford's brigade. Brigadier General William Wofford was in Kershaw's Division of Lt. General Richard Anderson's First Corps of the Army of Northern Virginia.

At about 5:00 p.m. on June 1, the Union Sixth Corps under Maj. General Horatio G. Wright prepared to meet the entrenched Confederates. Colonel Elisha Strong Kellogg ordered his green 2nd Connecticut Heavies up, dressed his line, and moved the men west to meet the rebels. Kellogg was in the 2nd Brigade under Brigadier General Emory Upton and included the 5th Maine, 121st New York, 95th and 96th Pennsylvania. Upton's men broke through the rebel defenses, turning Clingman's left and Wofford's right.

The breakthrough was short-lived. Colquitt's Georgians moved north of the New Cold Harbor Road to support Clingman. The 19th, 27th, and 28th Georgia regiments ran across a field, a distance of about 150 yards, to fill the gaps left by Clingman's men. Captain Keely said the 19th lost about forty-six men before they got into the trenches. As the men moved north, clearing the Federals out of the trenches, Keely captured a major in the 106th New York. The officer offered Keely his sword, while barely six feet away, a fellow Georgian raised his rifle to shoot the major. Keely hit the rifle with his sword, knocking the shot over the major's head. The Yankee prisoner was so thankful, he offered Keely a drink of whiskey from his canteen. The two men became good friends until Keely had him sent to the rear with the other prisoners.[2]

The Federal assault was repulsed, and the number of Yankees dead was staggering. In some parts of the field, men were stacked two or three high, where they fell dead on top of each other. Kellogg and fifty-two others in the 2nd Connecticut were dead, and 333 were wounded or missing. The regimental chaplain wrote, "You cannot conceive the horror and awfulness of a battle." The Heavies paid a tremendous price at Cold Harbor, but the men punched through the rebel defenses and made an advance further than any other regiment. The Sixth Corps had about 1,200 men killed and wounded, according to E. Porter Alexander.

The next day, June 2, was relatively quiet for the 19th Georgia with sporadic sharpshooting and artillery fire. The action had moved to the far left of the Confederate line, where Gen. Jubal Early made an attempt to turn the Union right flank. The Union troops across from Hoke's division made good use of the break in action to improve their works. A member of the 23rd Georgia in Colquitt's Brigade wrote, "The enemy is improving his ditch, and we annoy him as much as possible."[3]

On June 3, Grant ordered an attack all along the front at first light. Soon the rebel pickets were driven in by the advancing Yankees. The fire was furious as the blue-clad soldiers were falling at a rapid pace, but on and on they came. There was hand-to-hand fighting as the two armies became entangled in the battle's main event. Clubbed muskets and bayonets were the weapons of choice in such close fighting. The rebel yell and the Yankee huzzah could be heard up and down the line of battle. Some of the heaviest fighting of the day occurred at the southern end of the line. Barlow's division broke

---

2 *Atlanta Constitution* article, March 15, 1931.

3 Ernest B. Ferguson, *Not War but Murder: Cold Harbor 1864*, 132.

through the Confederate defenses briefly, only to be driven back by Joseph Finegan's Floridians and a battalion from Maryland.

In the book, *Fighting for the Confederacy* by E. Porter Alexander, there is a story about an artillery battalion assigned to Alexander to put in position on Hoke's line. The trenches did not always connect with the ones to the right or left, leaving some open ground between them. Alexander was trying to get the battalion in place, when he found himself not more than three hundred yards from the enemy line. A colonel nearby suggested Alexander wait until dark to make further movements as he was so close to the front line. He saw a breastwork about one hundred yards away and decided to make a run for it. He reached the work, jumped the parapet, and fell in the ditch, almost on General Colquitt. He said he had not met him before and that he barely had enough breath to introduce himself.[4]

Cold Harbor was Grant's greatest defeat. The number of Yankee casualties was staggering. A reporter in Hoke's line said of the scene in front of Colquitt's line "[he had] never seen as many dead in one place." A member of Colquitt's Brigade wrote, "I wouldn't believe it if I had not seen it, that we could kill so many hundreds with so slight a loss. After the enemy commence the charge, they don't fire."[5]

The rebels were convinced of the advantage of a well-constructed defensive position. Hoke's division was sent back to P. G. T. Beauregard at Petersburg as Lee was not sure of Grant's intentions in the days following Cold Harbor.

Grant had managed to maneuver his army south of the James River, in an effort to move around the right flank of the Confederates in Petersburg. E. Porter Alexander stated bluntly, "That was the time and place, the day and the hour, when the last hope of the Confederacy died down and flickered out." Alexander further stated the movement delayed Grant's capture of Petersburg by nine months. General Grant ordered William F. Smith to attack the Dimmock Line of Confederate entrenchments, south of Petersburg.

---

4 E. Porter Alexander, *Fighting for the Confederacy*, 412.

5 Ernest B. Ferguson, *Not War but Murder: Cold Harbor 1864*, 167.

Grant had overwhelming numbers in his favor with approximately fourteen thousand men against about 2,200 Confederates.[6]

The arrival of General Hoke's division prevented what might have been otherwise been a cake walk for Smith's troops in the capture of Petersburg. General Colquitt's brigade began digging trenches near Harrison's Creek, south of the Appomattox River. This was about the time the Federals were making an assault on the Petersburg Line under the command of Henry Wise. Colquitt's Georgians and Johnson Hagood's South Carolinians helped to stop the assault of Smith's men against Wise's Confederate troops over the following three days.

Another assault by Gershom Mott was ordered by Smith on June 18. Mott's men were ordered to assail the center of the Confederate line held by Colquitt's brigade. At 11:00 a.m., McAllister's brigade of Mott's division crossed the Prince George Court House Road to make the attack. The men moved about one hundred yards west and were met with a withering fire from the Georgians. According to McAllister, "Our ranks melted away."

Two additional brigades met the same fate as the attack was brought to a halt. About four-thirty in the afternoon, another assault was ordered by General George Meade. McAllister protested to Mott, but it was to no avail. The men of the 1st Maine Heavy Artillery climbed atop a road bank, dressed their line, and charged toward the Confederates. This attack met the same fate as the previous ones.

Out of nine hundred men in the 1st Maine Heavy Artillery, 632 were lost in the assault. The casualties suffered by the "Heavies" were the highest suffered by a regiment in either army over the entire four years.[7] From June 15–18, the Union Army suffered about 10,600 casualties in the ill-fated attempts to take Petersburg.[8]

Confederate losses were estimated to be between 2,970 and 4,700. While the losses suffered by the Confederate Army were much smaller numerically, the percentage of losses were much greater. It

---

6 Earl J. Hess, *In the Trenches at Petersburg*, 18.

7 Ibid., 34.

8 Ibid., 37.

has been estimated that Union troops outnumbered the Southerners, nine to one. With the continued building of blue-clad soldiers in his front, Johnston began pulling his men back to an interior line closer to Petersburg. The distance from the previous location was about eight hundred yards. Once in position, the men began to dig with whatever they could find. For the next three months, this new position would be home for the 19th Georgia and the rest of Hoke's brigade.

Life in the trenches around Petersburg was filled with monotony. Adjunct George H. Moffett from the 25th South Carolina may have said it best:

> Seldom are men called upon to endure as much as was required of the troops who occupied the trenches of Petersburg during the months of June, July and August. It was endurance without relief; sleeplessness without excitement; inactivity without rest; constant apprehension requiring ceaseless watching.[9]

On June 23, the Federal artillery began shelling the city. General Lee formulated a plan designed to dislodge the Union troops. General P. G. T. Beauregard outlined the plans for the offensive to his officers. Lee wanted to hit the Federal line between the Appomattox River and City Point Road. He chose this section based on his assessment that the Union line was weakest at this sector. General E. Porter Alexander was to enfilade the Union line with his artillery for about thirty minutes, beginning at 7:00 a.m. The engagement began right on time. General Robert Hoke and General Charles Field understood their duties differently. Each was under the impression they were to engage only after the other had begun. As a result, the attack was delayed.

Hoke feared the delay had given the enemy ample time to make preparations to receive the attack. Hoke did send in Hagood's bri-

---

9 Daniel Barefoot, *General Robert F. Hoke: Lee's Modest Warrior*, 214.

gade, but it was too little, too late. Hagood suffered considerable casualties.

General Lee was on hand to watch the attack. Following the failed attack, Lee commented there appeared to be a misunderstanding on the part of each division. General Grant began making a number of attempts to end the stalemate at Petersburg. Lieutenant Colonel Henry Pleasants Jr. from the 48th Pennsylvania was a civil engineer. His unit had a number of men who were coal miners before the war. He convinced Gen. Ambrose Burnside that with some help, he and his men could dig a mine under the Confederate line. He believed the mine could be filled with enough black powder to allow the Union troops to break through the gap made, once the powder was detonated.

Burnside was convinced the plan might work. He persuaded George Meade and, ultimately, General Grant. Work on the mine began right away. Dirt was moved, night and day, in preparation for the big explosion.

The Confederates became aware that something was up and began digging a countermine. Captain Thomas Abercrombie from Company I, known as the Villa Rica Gold Diggers, 19th Georgia was assigned to the engineers charged with digging the countermine. The name for the unit stemmed from the discovery of gold in the small community of Villa Rica in Carroll County, Georgia, in the 1840s.

The Yankees lit the fuse to their mine at 4:15 a.m. on July 30. The location of the black powder-filled cavity was directly under the 18th and 22nd South Carolina. When the explosion erupted at 4:44 a.m., many of the South Carolinians were buried alive as they slept.

The blast moved one hundred thousand cubic feet of dirt and created a hole 125 feet long, fifty feet wide, and thirty feet deep. Captain John Keely said of the affair: "On July 30th, at early dawn, a terrific explosion occurred about 300 yards to our left, and we too discovered that a mine had been sprung right in our trench, blowing to atoms every man in 150 yards of the ditch." Once the men came to their senses and sprang to action, Keely called the scene "maddening in the extreme."

Captain John Anderson Richardson of Company C, the Palmetto Guards, provided a summary of some of the men from the 19th Georgia for a reunion. The document is in the Kenan Research Center at the Atlanta History Center.

Captain Richardson recalled Isham Rainey was killed when the mine exploded at Petersburg. He stated he saw Rainey fall dead at his feet, and that his sword belt was cut by shrapnel while bending over to examine Rainey.[10]

After the mine failed to produce any positive results for General Grant, he decided to maneuver Major General Winfield S. Hancock in a position to disrupt Weldon Railroad. The Confederates relied on the train to move supplies into the besieged city from Weldon, North Carolina. Hancock had his II Corps and two divisions of the X Corps under Major General David B. Birney for what is known as Grant's fourth offensive. The ensuing battle was known as the Second Battle of Deep Bottom followed by the Battle of Globe Tavern.

On August 18, at about 1:00 p.m., General P. G. T. Beauregard ordered Colquitt's Brigade to join Major General Henry Heth. Heth's division was under the command of Lieutenant General A. P. Hill's Third Army Corps. Heth is believed to be the one responsible for starting the Battle of Gettysburg.

The Union Army vastly outnumbered the Confederates. Heth knew he was outnumbered from the prisoners captured and had questions about the troop strength. In the face of a superior force, he kept Colquitt's men in reserve. The Georgians were sent back to Petersburg, once the main event was over on the 18th. The marching to and from the Battle of Globe Tavern meant Colquitt's men did not get much rest that day.

The Union Army under Gouverneur K. Warren had established a foothold on the Weldon Railroad. The next day, Major General William Mahone proposed a plan to extract the Federals from this vital supply line. Heth planned to attack the Yankees straight down the railroad. Mahone would take his men and two brigades from

---

[10] Palmetto Guard Papers, Kenan Research Center, Atlanta History Center, #70-127-1.

Robert F. Hoke's division to hit the right rear of the V Corps. While Heth kept the Federals pinned down in the front, Mahone was to attack from the right flank and rear. The two brigades from Hoke were Colquitt's and Clingman's.

Shortly after noon on August 19, Colquitt's men were in the lead position, followed by Clingman's North Carolinians and David A. Weisiger's Virginians. Once all were in position, a line of battle was formed with Colquitt on the left, Clingman on the right, and Weisiger's men behind Colquitt in column. Mahone had the troops march west, across Vaughn Road, toward Weldon Railroad. The men smashed into the right flank of the Union line. The 19th Indiana caught a glimpse of the Southerners, when they were about twenty yards away. The dense underbrush hampered visibility at any great distance.

Colquitt's Georgians drove the old "Iron Brigade" of the 6th Wisconsin while Clingman's men rolled up the Hartshorne's Seven Shooters. The 191st and 190th Pennsylvanians were nearly surrounded. The men destroyed their rifles and then surrendered. Mahone's men kept up the pressure on the retreating Federals as they rounded up countless prisoners.

The weather on August 19, was not pleasant. Rain fell—sometimes quite hard—most of the day. The woods north of Globe Tavern and east of Weldon Railroad were covered in thick undergrowth. The dense vegetation, coupled with the rain, made it difficult for the men to keep their bearings. In a reunion speech given by General Colquitt, printed in the *Newnan Times-Herald* on October 30, 1874, he told a rather humorous story about Colonel Neal of the 19th Georgia.

Colquitt said when they marched to Weldon Railroad, they were somewhat confused and seemed lost. The day was dark and cloudy, and it was difficult to distinguish object more than one hundred yards distance. The brigade found it was between two lines of the enemy. The objective was to attack one of the lines and stay out of the way of the other.

"The coolness of the commander of the 19th Georgia was remarkable, and a braver, more gallant or loyal man never marched than Colonel Neal," Colquitt said. While going through the woods with one hundred men, he was suddenly confronted by a line of Federals four hundred strong. To cover the smaller number of his force, he called for his men to lay down. He then called for the Federal commander to surrender. The Federal officer replied, asking Neal to surrender. They eventually agreed to move along together, and whatever command they came in front of first would determine the victor.

As they marched along, trying to find their way back to their respective commands, they conversed freely. They condemned the harsh treatment of prisoners. They came in front of Confederates, and the Federal officer had to surrender. He said the first command given to the newly captured prisoners was "Stack arms," followed by "Take off that hat" and "Take off them shoes."

The entire brigade captured five silk flags and 2,500 men.[11]

The chaos that prevailed in the thick woods and undergrowth made for a trying time for the men on both sides. A member of the 51st North Carolina in Clingman's brigade mentioned that some of the men in his regiment were captured and recaptured several times.

Once Colquitt's and Clingman's brigades emerged from the woods, they had more prisoners than they had men in their respective brigades. General John F. Hartranft from Wilcox's division of the IX Corps opened fire on Colquitt's left as the rebels were entering Davis's cornfield from the woods.

Hartranft's men drove the Georgians out of the cornfield, into the timber on the northeastern edge of the clearing. In a short period, the Georgians in Colquitt's brigade rallied and countercharged the Yankees. North and south—both fired away at each other about seventy-five yards apart. It could be here that Willis P. Menefee of Company C was killed. According to Captain Richardson, Menefee was killed at the Battle of Weldon Railroad while standing on a breastwork, firing at the enemy. This encounter was brief, and the Georgians withdrew again once Colonel William Humphrey's Second Brigade arrived in support of Hartranft.

---

[11] *Newnan Times-Herald*, October 30, 1874.

Colquitt's men made it back to the Confederate lines. Colquitt's troops and Clingman's brigades had almost wiped out three Federal brigades and severely abused two more.

Mahone caught a glimpse of Colquitt returning to the lines and rode out to meet him. He asked General Colquitt what happened to rest of his brigade. Colquitt pointed to about 150 men and said, "These are all I have left."[12]

The attempt to dislodge the Federals from the railroad lasted three days. Despite some hard fighting and small pockets of victory, the attempt failed. Following the battle of Weldon Railroad, the 19th Georgia went back to the trenches in and around Petersburg. On September 28, General Hoke was ordered to take his division north, across the James River. That same day, Grant had successfully captured Fort Harrison. General Lee believed his men could recapture Fort Harrison and made plans to do so on September 30.

General Hoke was not on board with Lee's plans. He believed the endeavor was impractical and would result in an unnecessary loss of life. He informed Colquitt and Clingman of their roles in the assault. He gave the command for the men to advance at the appointed time. The men advanced but were repulsed. General Lee urged Hoke to advance again, which he did, resulting in the same outcome.

Following the Fort Harrison debacle, General Lee left Hoke's division north of the James River for the following three months. During that time, the men were to occupy the trenches between Darbytown and the Charles City Roads. General Lee decided to attempt to retake a portion of the line occupied by Grant's troops. The attack was to begin at dawn on October 7 with General Fields and Hoke's brigades.

It is not clear if General Hoke fully understood his role in the action of October 7. According to one account, his division was to be held in reserve. General Field was under the impression that Hoke was to move at the same time as his division in the attempt to turn

---

[12] John Horn, *The Siege of Petersburg: The Battles for the Weldon Railroad, August 1864.*

the left flank of the Union line. For reasons unknown, Hoke did not move.

E. Porter Alexander, in his book *Fighting for the Confederacy*, specifically says on page 483, "Hoke's line on his [Field's] right never moved. I never knew why."

During the remaining time around Richmond and Petersburg, the men had to endure the daily grind associated with trench warfare. Captain Anderson said in the papers referenced above that the regiment lost several men in the trenches. He said if a hand or a foot were exposed above the trench, it would draw immediate fire from the enemy. He recalled the time a ramrod was shot through the hat of one of the troops.

On December 9, 1864, Hoke received orders to move his division south to Wilmington, North Carolina, in defense of Fort Fisher. The fort was one of the last open to the blockade runners and a primary source of supplies for Lee's army. The Army of Northern Virginia desperately needed the supplies received in Wilmington. On December 20, Hoke's men were ordered to draw three days rations to prepare for relocating at a moment's notice. It wasn't long before the notice came in the form of a line of march to the railroad in Richmond. Captain John Keely reported that at dark, they boarded the cars on the journey to Wilmington. The weather around Richmond at the time was anything but hospitable. Freezing rain made the trip miserable beyond belief. According to Keely, nine men froze to death on the way.

CHAPTER 11

Fort Fisher

In the final months of 1864, the 19th Georgia was enduring life in the trenches around Petersburg, Virginia. At the same time, the Union was looking at options on how best to curtail the blockade running and ultimately stop the flow of supplies to the Army of Northern Virginia. The last major port open to blockade runners at this stage of the war was Wilmington, North Carolina, some 250 miles south of Petersburg. The city was protected by several forts on the coast and on the banks of the Cape Fear River from New Inlet, all the way to the city docks. The largest was Fort Fisher located on Confederate Point, the finger of land that separated the Cape Fear River from the Atlantic Ocean.

Fort Fisher was a massive mound of sand in the shape of the number "7" with the longest part facing the Atlantic, and the top part facing north, toward Wilmington. The fort had an assortment of artillery placed on batteries along the sea face and land face. The palisade stretched across the island east and west, from the Cape Fear River to the ocean.

Fort Fisher was named for Charles Fredrick Fisher, the very popular colonel of the 6th North Carolina infantry killed at the First Battle of Manassas in July 1861. The size of the fort earned it the name "Confederate Goliath." The commander was Colonel William Lamb from the 36th North Carolina Regiment. He was a trained engineer and, by all accounts, did an excellent job of fortifying the earthen fort.

In these final months of the war, the Confederate Army was running short on troops and everything else needed to stay in the fight for Southern independence. The shortage of troops meant Colonel Lamb commanded his massive fort substantially undermanned. He initially had only six hundred troops in the garrison.

The troops manning the fort were primarily the 36th North Carolina, and the men had no real combat experience. As rumors of a Union attack continued to filter down to the port at Wilmington and the fort, Lamb sent countless requests for more troops. After a large Union fleet was spotted off the coast in December, reinforcements were sent to Lamb, made up of the two companies of the 10th North Carolina Artillery and the 7th Battalion of Junior Reserves. The Junior Reserves were comprised of teenagers.

Major General William Henry Chase Whiting was the commander of the Cape Fear District, which included Fort Fisher. Whiting continued to request reinforcements for Wilmington and Fort Fisher from the Confederate War Department. General Lee thought the threat to the port was exaggerated. Besides, Lee needed every available man in the defense of Petersburg.

Once the buildup of Union vessels was spotted off the coast by lookouts at Fort Fisher, Robert E. Lee agreed to send General Robert Hoke's division to Wilmington. The division consisted of 6,500 troops, and the orders to move south in defense of the valuable port were issued on or about December 17.

Robert Hoke's division was comprised of seasoned combat veterans, and Lamb and Whiting were pleased to hear the much-needed reinforcements were en route. Union activity between Wilmington and Petersburg made Hoke's trip difficult and dangerous. Destroyed railroad tracks, overused locomotives in need of repairs and maintenance added to the difficulty of moving the reinforcements. In addition, the weather did not cooperate with the excursion. Hoke's men were battered with sleet, freezing rain, snow, and freezing temperatures.

The first of Hoke's division under Brigadier General William Kirkland arrived in Wilmington at midnight on December 23. His brigade was directed to the Sugar Loaf Line upon arrival. The defensive line was a fortified earthwork, about four and a half miles north of Fort Fisher that ran east to west.

At 2:10 p.m. on December 25, Brevet Brigadier General N. Martin Curtis from the First Brigade, second division, XXIV Army Corps Department of Virginia and North Carolina, planted a flag on the beach at the Union landing site. The rest of the infantry would follow in launches from the Navy ships in and around the drop zone. The federal landing was uncontested by the Confederate defenders.

In the city, Christmas Day church services were being held while the bombardment of Fort Fisher on Confederate Point was in full swing. What a paradox of activity with the citizens of Wilmington, worshipping the birth of the Prince of Peace while just down the peninsula, their fellow men were trying to kill each other.

This first attempt to take Fort Fisher by the Union did not garner the success hoped for by US officials, from President Lincoln down the chain of command. Even though the troops captured some Confederate prisoners and inflicted some casualties, Butler lost his nerve. His lead division got to within a mile and a half of Fort Fisher. Observers did not see the expected destruction of the fort by the countless shells thrown at it by the US Navy bombardment. Instead, they saw a well-fortified position and Confederate gunners eagerly awaiting their arrival.

Butler found out about the arrival of Hoke's division from captured prisoners. He became concerned about being caught in the middle between the fort to the south and the Sugar Loaf Line to the north and the ocean to the east. Despite the disapproval of his subordinate commanders, Butler ordered a retreat. The Union abandoned the expedition, and the ships headed north.

The remaining troops in Hoke's division did not reach Wilmington until December 26. In fact, Captain John Keely from the 19th Georgia remarked in an article published in 1931 by the *Atlanta Journal* that their arrival in Wilmington was too late. He was right—the division was too late—not because the Union attack had been called off and the men extracted from Confederate Point but because the Federal Army had a good opportunity for reconnaissance.

Many of Butler's officers believed the fort could have been taken. There was one more challenge the Confederates had to deal with in the defense of Fort Fisher and, ultimately, Wilmington, and that was Braxton Bragg. As the threat of an invasion by Union forces became increasingly apparent, the Confederate high command began to have second thoughts about Whiting's abilities as a commander. In October 1864, General Bragg was sent to Wilmington to take over command. General Whiting was relegated to Bragg's second in command. It was the belief of many in the Confederacy that Bragg was an incompetent general. His past performance in the western theater of the war and other engagements were the basis of this sentiment. At the second Battle of Fort Fisher, Bragg once again proved his detractors were correct in their assessment of his performance as a general.

His friendship with President Davis was Bragg's lifeline. Following the withdrawal of the Union troops from Confederate Point, there was much celebration of the "victory" by the troops. General Bragg ordered a grand review of the troops to celebrate the victory. On January 8, 1865, Hoke's division was ordered to participate in a dress parade before the division was sent back to Virginia.

On January 12, Colonel Lamb spotted the return of US ships off the coast. The Yankees were back to try again to close the port at Wilmington. This time, the outcome was substantially different from the previous attempt. The Union Army overwhelmed the defenders of the massive fort, beginning with a bombardment that landed nearly 19,682 shells in and around the site. Following the shelling at 3:25 p.m., the warships let loose a blast from the steam whistles in unison to signal the ground attack was to commence.[1]

Colonel Lamb and General Whiting pleaded with Bragg for reinforcements to fend off the pending attack. When no reinforcements arrived, the men came to realize the fort must be sacrificed. The Yankees landed more than four thousand troops on the beach,

---

1 Chris E. Fonvielle Jr., *The Wilmington Campaign: Last Rays of Departing Hope.*

north of the fort. The battle was a bloody affair. Both armies fought diligently to thwart the other's attacks. In the end, the Union Army had the advantage in numbers and the fort was captured on January 15, 1865. General Bragg sent General Colquitt to take over command of the fort. He found Lamb and Whiting, both wounded, holed up at Battery Buchanan. Lamb begged Colquitt to convince Bragg to attempt a counterattack to retake to fort. In the middle of this exchange, the leading units of the Federal Army approached the battery. Colquitt had no choice other than make a hasty exit or be captured.

The 19th Georgia was at Sugar Loaf with the rest of Hoke's division, awaiting orders from General Bragg. Sugar Loaf was a line of earthworks, north of Fort Fisher, stretching from the Cape Fear River, east, to the Atlantic Ocean. Colquitt's brigade was positioned closest to the river. Hoke mistakenly believed the Federals landing on the beach planned to march north and attack Wilmington.[2]

With that belief in mind, he held a defensive posture. Many of the troops could not understand why Hoke did not attack the troops landing to his east. No doubt General Alfred Terry's troops were the most vulnerable as they tried to carve out a piece of shoreline to unload troops and instruments of war. Unopposed, the men filtered south, toward Fort Fisher.

Their destination was between Fort Fisher and Sugar Loaf in a line facing south, only a few miles from the fort. Lamb and Whiting anticipated Bragg would have Hoke attack the rear of the advancing Federals. It is not known why Bragg did not have Hoke's men attack the Federal troops positioned between Sugar Loaf and Fort Fisher. Having received no such orders, the men remained behind the earthwork while Fort Fisher fell.

Captain Keely mentioned in his diary that the men made a few "desperate stands" at Sugar Loaf. He further stated that Hoke's men skirmished with the enemy every day while they were on the peninsula. It was not until the US Navy gunboats maneuvered up the Cape

---

2 Ibid., 214.

Fear River far enough to shell the Confederate trenches that the order was given to withdraw.

Captain Keely described the ordeal as follows: "The enemy fleet came up the river, and, getting on our right flank, opened up a perfect hurricane of shot and shell upon us." In the days following the capture of the fort, the Yankees took time to care for the wounded and bury the dead. The Federal losses from the battle totaled between 1,166 and 1,452.[3] Confederate losses came to about five hundred killed or wounded and about 1,400 taken prisoner.

---

[3] Ibid., 306.

CHAPTER 12

Kinston and Bentonville

On February 22, 1865, Wilmington, North Carolina, surrendered to General Terry. That same day, President Jefferson Davis appointed Joseph Johnston to command the Army of Tennessee. On February 23, General Hoke had his troops at Rockfish Creek, about twenty-five miles north of Wilmington. With no sign of pursuit from the Union Army, the rebels enjoyed about ten days of rest.

On March 5, Hoke was ordered to Kinston, North Carolina, to delay the movement of Major General Jacob D. Cox. Johnston believed if he could keep Sherman—approaching from the south—from uniting with General Schofield and General Terry—in and around Wilmington—he might have a chance for a victory.

General Cox had been sent to New Berne with a division of the XXIII Corps because of the lack of sufficient capacity on the cars from Wilmington. Cox had an estimated thirteen thousand troops under his command. He was ordered to join with the Union garrison stationed at New Berne.

Once the troops were consolidated, they were to coordinate with General Schofield and converge on Goldsboro, Cox from the east and Schofield from the southeast. The condition of the rails made Cox's advance somewhat difficult. His concern was for his supplies traveling by rail inland.

General Bragg became aware of Cox's advance toward Kinston from New Berne and sent a request to General Johnston for additional troops. Johnston approved the request and agreed to send General Daniel Harvey Hill and his two thousand troops stationed at Smithville. Johnston hoped Bragg could keep Cox from reaching General Sherman.

Hoke's division reached Kinston on March 6. He immediately had his men start entrenching around Southwest Creek, a tributary of the Neuse River. On March 7, Cox had his Federals move up to Wise's Forks. That night, General Hoke met with Generals Bragg and D. H. Hill to discuss strategy for an attack on Cox. Hoke had a plan to catch the Federals by surprise and potentially land a crushing blow.

General Hill had his troops in Kinston on the evening of March 7. He ordered his men to relieve Hoke's men in the trenches at Southwest Creek. Hoke was to take his men and move around the left flank of the Union Army. By 8:00 a.m. on March 8, Cox was about three miles from Kinston. He met with General Schofield around nine to discuss the crossing of Southwest Creek.

General Cox was made aware of a large number of Confederates crossing the creek in the early morning hours. Cox ignored the warning. At the sound of Hoke's guns, Hill was to have his men leave the trenches and cross the creek, south of Hoke. The plan was to have Hill in position to cut off the Federal's line of retreat.

Hoke's attack was concentrated on the 15th Connecticut. Hill routed the 17th Massachusetts. The heavy fire from Hoke and Hill had a demoralizing effect on the Federals. With men falling on every side, the 15th Connecticut surrendered and the regiment ceased to exist. By the end of the day, Hoke's men had captured more than one thousand prisoners.[1]

The 19th Georgia lost Colonel James Neal at the engagement at Kinston. According to Captain Keely, "Colonel Neal fell, shot through the brain while, with his usual gallantry, and sword in his hand, he was in the front of the regiment—leading it on."[2]

---

1 Daniel W. Barefoot, *General Robert F. Hoke: Lee's Modest Warrior*, 287.

2 *Atlanta Constitution* article.

On March 9 and 10, Hoke was ordered to make another attempt to turn Cox's left. The maneuver was at first promising but, as with most of the engagements led by Bragg, it failed. It is believed by many that Bragg doomed the attack when he sent Hill's troops on a separate mission, rather than devoting his entire force in the defeat of General Cox.

Following the defeat at Wise Forks/Kinston, Bragg was ordered to Smithfield, located about midway between Raleigh and Goldsboro. Hoke's troops arrived in Smithfield on March 16. As the men went into camp about two miles south of town, they were given some much-needed rest on March 17. Hoke's division numbered about 4,775, including about eight hundred former artillery men converted to infantry.[3]

On March 18, General Hoke had his men up and ready to march by 9:00 a.m. Almost fifteen miles due south of Smithfield is the small community of Bentonville. This little community in North Carolina would be the location of the final battle fought by the 19th Georgia and the rest of the Confederacy.

Once the men were in Bentonville, they had to camp on wet ground with orders to build no fires. Johnston still hoped to surprise the lead division of Sherman's troops, marching east on the Goldsboro Road. March 19 dawned sunny and clear. "A more beautiful morning I never saw," commented a private in the 89th Ohio.

General Wade Hampton's cavalry did an excellent job of screening the movement of the Confederate troops from the enemy. Once in position at the far left of the Confederate line, General Hoke ordered his men to begin building works as he understood his role was as a blocking force.

The 19th Georgia was positioned just to the south of the Goldsboro Road, facing west. The far left was anchored by Kirkland's brigade. To his right were Hagood's troops. To the right of Hagood was Colquitt's brigade, led by Colonel Charles Zachry. To the right of Colquitt was the North Carolina Junior Reserves, and to Colquitt's rear was Clingman's brigade.

---

3 Nathaniel C. Hughes Jr., *Bentonville: The Final Battle of Sherman and Johnston*, 40.

The Confederate battle line looked like a sickle with the handle running north to south and the blade arching from east to west. Hoke's division was at the bottom of the handle. Just to the south of the line was a swampy area considered to be semi-impassable.

The Union soldiers were marching into Johnston's trap. The lead division of the General Slocum's XIV Corps was that of William Passmore Carlin. Carlin's 1st brigade was that of Colonel Harrison Hobart, followed by the 2nd brigade under General George P. Buell, and the 3rd was under the command of Colonel David Miles.

Skirmishers had seen the Confederates—Hampton's cavalry—much of the morning. Reports of rebels to the front were dismissed as only cavalry. As the Union skirmishers ran into heavier resistance, it was determined that what might lie ahead was more than cavalry. Hobart instructed his men to veer off to the left of the Goldsboro Road followed by Buell. These troops moved north, toward the arch of the sickle formation. David Miles' troops went to the right of the Goldsboro Road and ran into General Hoke's men behind partially completed breastworks.

The 104th Indiana, the 21st Ohio, the 38th Indiana, and the 79th Pennsylvania were facing east, toward Hoke's division. The Union soldiers charged the breastworks again and again with heavy losses. The ferocity of the attack by the Federals was such that Bragg called for reinforcements. Carlin as well sent word to Slocum that the rebel line was more than cavalry.

Hoke's line repulsed the enemy with each renewed attack. If the reinforcements ordered by Bragg had made it to the fight, there might have been a different outcome. McLaws was sent to reinforce Hoke's left, but mistakes made by his guide and conflicting orders did not provide Hoke with the full benefit of McLaws' brigade.

After two attacks from Miles, General Bragg ordered Hoke to have his men charge the Federals. Following orders, the men prepared to charge. It was at this moment the last great charge of the war made by the doomed Confederacy took place.

An officer in Slocum's command said, "The Rebel regiments in front were in full view, stretching to the left as far as one could see, advancing rapidly, and firing as they came. It was a gallant sight." The rebel yell rose from the throats of men unwilling to admit defeat.

According to Captain Keely, the Confederates got to within about sixty yards of the enemy as he was hit in the leg by a bullet. The wound was just above his ankle, and it would trouble him for the remainder of his life.

As darkness began to settle over the field, the day's fight came to a close. The wounded were placed into ambulances to be transported to Smithfield. The Bentonville-Smithfield Road was corduroyed, making the trip horrific for the wounded. One of the passengers climbed out the wagon, found a horse, and rode on to Smithfield, even though his arm had recently been amputated. Captain Keely, in the article written by the *Atlanta Constitution*, mentioned the excruciating pain from his wound, and the bumpy ride in the wagon making it even worse. The wounded were then loaded into railcars and sent to Raleigh.

In the early morning hours of March 20, Johnston had his left wing, Hoke, swing back to his left, 120 degrees. Once the maneuver was complete, the men began to entrench again. Johnston's movements were more defensive in that he had to both protect his flanks and keep his escape route open. He knew that Union reinforcements had him severely outnumbered.

In his current position, Johnston was facing Oliver Otis Howard's and Henry Slocum's men, including the 20th Corps of William on the far left, Jefferson C. Davis's 14th Corps to the right of Williams, Logan's 15th Corps was next, followed by the 17th Corps of Blair on the far right.

General Sherman hoped that Johnston would withdraw. The Federals attacked Hoke and McLaws on the left of Johnston's line a number of times. Some of the attacks were repulsed, some were not, and it was back and forth all afternoon on March 20. Johnston withdrew and moved his men back north of Bentonville and across Mill Creek.

Reports on the number of casualties suffered by the 19th Georgia and the rest of Hoke's men vary. In his book, Bentonville: The final Battle of Sherman and Johnston, Nathaniel C. Hughes

Jr. reported Colquitt's losses at forty killed and 177 wounded. In the book *Battle of Despair*, by Robert P. Broadwater, Hoke's loss was listed at 740 men. There is one more reference that reported Colquitt's Georgians—led by Zachary—suffered the worst with thirty-three killed, 163 wounded, and eighteen missing.

General Johnston had high hopes of defeating the left wing of Sherman's army on its northward march through the Carolinas. Johnston relied on a strategy of luring the enemy further and further in his direction. He hoped to stretch the Union troops to a weak point and then attack. Johnston had employed the same strategy at Seven Pines and, again, in Atlanta.

Despite initial success at Bentonville, Johnston was just outnumbered. He realized the odds were not in his favor and made the retreat to Smithfield. Sherman did not pursue Johnston aggressively in the retreat.

Perhaps Johnston knew the end was in sight, and it was just a matter of time. Soaking rains over the previous few days had turned the roads into muddy quagmires. The retreat was slow and difficult. Hoke's men served as rear guard on the retreat. They arrived at camp about 2:00 a.m. on March 22. The men finally got an opportunity to rest and think about the recent events.

The 19th Georgia remained with General Hoke in Smithfield. On April 4, the men stood at attention for a review by General Johnston. On April 5, rumors began to spread of the fall of Richmond. On April 10, Johnston ordered Hoke and his men to prepare for what would be their final march in the Confederate Army.

On April 11, the division marched about fifteen miles and bivouacked about five miles east of Raleigh. The following day, the men marched through Raleigh and on about seven miles to what is now known as Cary, North Carolina.[4]

Captain Keely from Company B, 19th Georgia, was recovering from his wound suffered at Bentonville in Raleigh. He had his attendant put his bed close to the window so he could see the old 19th

---

[4] Daniel W. Barefoot, *General Robert F. Hoke: Lee's Modest Warrior*, 309.

Georgia as they moved through town. When the men saw the captain, they gave him a cheer and shouted, "Goodbye, Captain Keely."

The news of General Lee's surrender on April 9 began to filter down to the rank and file of the Confederate Army. Sherman and Johnston negotiated a surrender of the troops in North Carolina on April 26, 1865.

The fighting was over. Many young men who joined up with the 19th Georgia in 1861 did not come home. Those who survived the war went home forever changed—with lasting memories of comrades and battles and deprivation. The reunited United States was also changed, forever impacted by a war that refuses to be forgotten.

Included in this photo are several officers in Company C 19th Georgia. The man in the center with the sword is believed to be Major Andrew J. Hutchens, next to him is Lieutenant Colonel Thomas Johnson's wife holding the hand of her husband. Standing behind Hutchens is Lieutenant William Johnson. Photo taken near Richmond in June 1862.

This picture of the 19th Georgia flag was issued much later in the war. It is on display at the Museum of Southern History in Jacksonville, FL.

Brigadier General Alfred H. Colquitt. Photo from Kerry Elliott collection.

Captain John Keely Co. B. Photo provided by Kathy Keely Smith

Captain Keely's grave Oakland Cemetery Atlanta, GA Photo by author

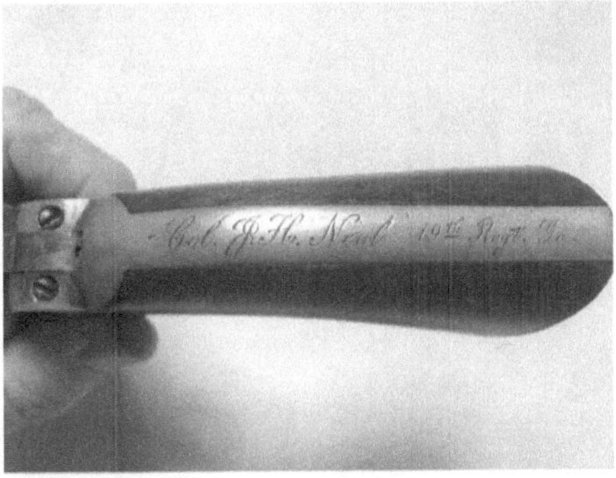

Colonel James H. Neal's revolver in the Kerry Elliott collection photo provided by Kerry Elliott

Tilghman W. Flynt Co G and his wife Martha Jane Turner Flynt with family. Photo taken in Griffin, GA 1906. Provided by Eric Flynt

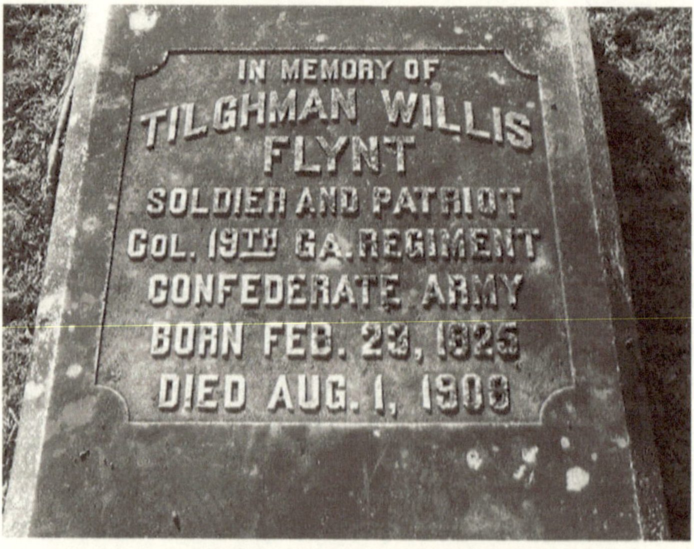

Colonel Flynt's Grave Oak Hill Cemetery
Griffin, GA Provided by Eric Flynt

Colonel James H. Neal's grave Oakland Cemetery
Atlanta, GA photo by author

John R. Carmichael Co. G

Company D Reunion 1909 provided by Sam Pyle

Isham Morris Co. I photo provided by Sam Pyle

The 19th Georgia member furthest from home is Captain A. J. Kennedy Co. F. He is buried in Inangahua Junction Cemetery, Inangahua Junction, Butler District, West Coast, New Zealand. Photo provided by Joanne Black.

Private J. D. Holcombe Co. F. Photo provided by John Hill SCV Camp 2087

Private James Freeman Walker Company F. Photo provided by Sam Pyle

Private John Wesley Walker Co. F. Photo provided by Sam Pyle

Private Moses Morris Co. I. Photo provided by Sam Pyle

BIBLIOGRAPHY

Alexander, E. Porter. *Fighting for the Confederacy*. Edited by Gary W. Gallager. Chapel Hill: The University of North Carolina Press, 1989.

Alexander, Russell A., and David J. Coles. *The Confederate Roll of Honor: Southern Casualties at the Battle of Olustee*. 1997.

Antietam National Battlefield Staff. Sharpsburg, Maryland.

Atlanta Constitution Magazine. March 15, 1931. Article on Captain John Keely Diary.

Atlanta History Center, Kenan Research Center, Atlanta, Georgia. Keely File, Palmetto Guards Papers by John Anderson Richardson, August 1912, and Menefee Timmons Papers (notes taken by Keith S. Bohannon).

Barefoot, Daniel W. *General Robert F. Hoke: Lee's Modest Warrior*. North Carolina: John F. Blair Publisher, 1996.

Beall, John B. *In Barrack and Field: Poems and Sketches of Army Life*. Smith & Lamar, Agents Publishing House of the M. E. Church, South Nashville, Tennessee, Dallas, Texas.

Beall Letters. University of North Carolinaz Chapel Hill, Special Collections.

Bowers, William A. *The 27th Georgia Volunteer Infantry Regiment*. Self-published. Global Authors Publications, 2014.

Bradshaw, Timothy W. Jr. *Battery Wagner: The Siege, the Men Who Fought, and the Casualties*. South Carolina: Palmetto Historical Works, 1993.

Broadwater, Robert P. *The Battle of Olustee, 1864: The Final Union Attempt to Seize Florida*. North Carolina and London: McFarland & Company, Inc.

Broadwater, Robert Paul. *Battle of Despair: Bentonville and the North Carolina Campaign*. Georgia: Mercer University Press, 2004.

Bryant, James K. II. *The Battle of Fredericksburg: We Cannot Escape History*. South Carolina: History Press, 2010.

Coffman, Richard M., and Kurt D. Graham. *To Honor these Men: A History of the Phillips Georgia Legion Infantry Battalion*, Georgia: Mercer University Press, 2007.

Digital Library of Georgia. Georgia Historic Newspapers. University of Georgia.

Dooley, Vincent Joseph, and Samuel Norman Thomas Jr. *The Legion's Fighting Bulldog*. Georgia: Mercer University Press, 2017.

Dowdey, Clifford. *The Seven Days: The Emergence of Lee*. Nebraska: University of Nebraska, 1964.

Fitzpatrick, Marion Hill. Edited by Jeffery C. Lowe and Sam Hodges. *Letters to Amanda*. Georgia: Mercer University Press, 1998.

Fletcher, William A. *Rebel Private: Front and Rear—Memoirs of a Confederate Soldier*. Meridian Books, 1995.

Fold 3. ancestry.com, Military Records.

Folsom, James Madison. *Heroes and Martyrs of Georgia—Georgia's Record in the Revolution of 1861*. Burke, Boykin & Company, 1864, New Material 1995.

Fonvielle, Chris E. Jr. *The Wilmington Campaign: Last Rays of Departing Hope*. Pennsylvania: Stackpole Books, 1997.

Fox, John J. III. *Red Clay to Richmond: Trail of the 35th Georgia Infantry Regiment, C. S. A.* Angle Valley Press, 2004.

Fredericksburg Battlefield Staff. Fredericksburg, Virginia.

Fulton, William Frierson Jr. *Family Record and War Reminiscences*. Livingston, Alabama, 1919.

Furgurson, Ernest B. *Not War but Murder: Cold Harbor 1864*. New York: Vintage Books, A Division of Random House, Inc., 2000.

Gallagher, Gary W. (Editor). *Chancellorsville: The Battle and Its Aftermath*. Chapel Hill and London: The University of North Carolina Press, 1996.

Georgia Archives. Special Collection Letters. D. D. Morris Civil War Letters, Joab Roach Letters, F. M. Hail Letters.

Gragg, Rod. *Confederate Goliath*. Harper Collins, 1991.

Gwynne, S. C. *Rebel Yell: The Violence, Passion, and Redemption of Stonewall Jackson*. Scribner, 2015.

Hassler, William Woods. *A. P. Hill: Lee's Forgotten General.* Chapel Hill: The University of North Carolina Press, 1957.

Hennessy, John J. *Return to Bull Run: The Campaign and Battle of Second Manassas*. Oklahoma: University of Oklahoma Press, 1993.

Hess, Earl J. *In the Trenches at Petersburg: Field Fortifications and Confederate Defeat*. Chapel Hill: The University of North Carolina Press, 2009.

Horn, John. *The Siege of Petersburg: The Battles for Weldon Railroad, August 1864*. California: Savas Beatie, 2015.

Hughes, Nathaniel Cheairs Jr. *Bentonville*. Chapel Hill and London: The University of North Carolina Press, 1996.

Krick, Robert K. *Stonewall Jackson at Cedar Mountain*. Chapel Hill: The University of North Carolina Press, 1990.

Korda, Michael. *The Life and Legend of Robert E. Lee*. Harper Perennial, 2015.

Mackowski, Chris, and Khristopher D. White. *Simply Murder: The Battle of Fredericksburg, December 13, 1862*. California: Savas Beatie, LLC, 2013, 2017.

Manassas Battlefield Staff. Manassas, Virginia.

Martin, David G. *The Second Bull Run Campaign: July–August 1862*. Pennsylvania: Combined Books, Inc., 1997.

Nichols, Gary D. *Hurrah for Georgia: The History of the 38th Georgia Regiment*. A 15 Publishing, 2017.

Nulty, William H. *Confederate Florida: The Road to Olustee*. Alabama: The University of Alabama Press, 1990.

O'Reilly, Francis Augustin. *The Fredericksburg Campaign, Winter War on the Rappahannock*. Baton Rouge: Louisiana State University Press, 2003.

Regimental Losses in the American Civil War, 1861–1865. A Treatise.

Reminiscences of the Boys in Gray, 1861–1865.

Rigdon, John C. *Historical Sketch and Roster of the Georgia 19th Infantry Regiment*. Georgia: Eastern Digital Resources, 2004.

Roddy, Ray. *The 11th Georgia Volunteer Infantry 1861–1865*. Nebraska: Morris Publishing, 1998.

Schenck, Martin. *Up Came Hill: The Story of the Light Division and Its Leaders*. Pennsylvania: The Stackpole Company, 1958.

Sears, Stephen W. *Landscape Turned Red: The Battle of Antietam*. Boston, New York: Houghton Mifflin Company, 1983.

Sears, Stephen W. *Chancellorsville*. Boston, New York: Houghton Mifflin Company, 1996.

Smedlund, William S. *Camp Fires of Georgia's Troops: 1861–1865*. Kennesaw Mountain Press, 1994.

Spruill, Matt III, and Matt Spruill IV. *Summer Lightning: A Guide to the Second Battle of Manassas*. Tennessee: University of Tennessee Press, 2013.

Taylor, Paul. *He Hath Loosed the Fateful Lightning: The Battle of Ox Hill (Chantilly) September 1, 1862*. Pennsylvania: White Main Books, 1959.

The War of the Rebellion: *A Compilation of the Official Records of the Civil War*. Time-Life Books, Voices of the Civil War.

University of North Carolina Wilson Library Archival and Manuscript Material. John Bramblett Beall Letters, 1860–1865.

Wilkerson, Warren, and Steven E. Woodworth. *A Scythe of Fire: A Civil War Story of the Eighth Georgia Infantry Regiment*. HarperCollins, 2002.

Wise, Stephen R. *Gate of Hell: Campaign for Charleston Harbor, 1863*. University of South Carolina Press, 1994.

Willingham, Ben H. *Florida in Turmoil: The Terrible War Years 1861–1865*. Osborn of Jackson, LLC, 2016.

Battlefield visits

Sharpsburg, Maryland, Manassas, Virginia

Beaver Dam Creek, Richmond, Virginia, Fredericksburg, Virginia, Chancellorsville, Virginia

Fort Sumter, Charleston, South Carolina, Olustee, Lake City, Florida

James Island, Charleston, South Carolina

ABOUT THE AUTHOR

Allan Payton is a lifelong resident of Newnan, Georgia. He received his degree in political science from the University of West Georgia in 1980. He has been a banker in metro Atlanta for the past forty-plus years. His love of history dates back to his childhood, listening to family stories told by his parents and grandparents. Allan and his wife, Paige, have four children and four grandchildren.

www.ingramcontent.com/pod-product-compliance
Lightning Source LLC
Chambersburg PA
CBHW021210160726
47994CB00001B/416